Fairy Tale Readers' Theater

10 Fairy Tales Rewritten as Readers' Theater Scripts for Struggling Readers to Improve Fluency and Comprehension Skills

by
Jo Browning Wroe

illustrated by
Julie Anderson

Publisher
Key Education Publishing Company, LLC
Minneapolis, Minnesota

www.keyeducationpublishing.com

CONGRATULATIONS ON YOUR PURCHASE OF A KEY EDUCATION PRODUCT!

The editors at Key Education are former teachers who bring experience, enthusiasm, and quality to each and every product. Thousands of teachers have looked to the staff at Key Education for new and innovative resources to make their work more enjoyable and rewarding. Key Education is committed to developing and publishing educational materials that will assist teachers in building a strong and developmentally appropriate curriculum for young children.

PLAN FOR GREAT TEACHING EXPERIENCES WHEN YOU USE
EDUCATIONAL MATERIALS FROM KEY EDUCATION PUBLISHING COMPANY, LLC

Credits

Authors:	Jo Browning Wroe
Publisher:	Sherrill B. Flora
Art Director:	Annette Hollister-Papp
Illustrator:	Julie Anderson
Editor:	Claude Chalk
Production:	Key Education Staff

Key Education welcomes manuscripts and product ideas from teachers. For a copy of our submission guidelines, please send a self-addressed, stamped envelope to:

Key Education Publishing Company, LLC
Acquisitions Department
9601 Newton Avenue South
Minneapolis, Minnesota 55431

About the Author of the Stories:

Jo Browning Wroe has taught both in the United Kingdom and in the United States. She earned her undergraduate degrees in English and Education from Cambridge University, Cambridge, England. She worked for twelve years in educational publishing before completing a Masters Degree in Creative Writing from the University of East Anglia, Norwich, England. Most of her time is now spent writing teacher resource materials and running workshops for others who love to write. Jo has been the recipient of the National Toy Libraries Award. She lives in Cambridge, England with her two daughters, Alice and Ruby, and her husband, John. This is the ninth book Jo Browning Wroe has written for Key Education.

Standard Book Number: 978-1-602680-43-2
High-Interest/Low Readability:
Fairy-Tale Readers' Theater
Copyright © 2009 by Key Education Publishing Company, LLC
Minneapolis, Minnesota 55431

Contents

Important Facts about the Scripts included in *Fairy Tale Readers' Theater*

1. **Entire Class Production:** Every fairy tale can become an "entire class production" when you use the "group readings" included in each script. The group readings are also excellent for shy children, English language learners, and struggling readers. Reading in a group can help these children feel more self-confident while increasing their language skills and fluency.

2. **Small Group Readings:** Every fairy tale can become a "small group production" by simply eliminating the group readings. Make a single copy of the script and "white-out" the group reading lines. Then, copy the edited script for the remaining story characters. Eliminating the "group readings" will not alter or detract from the original story.

3. **Specific Reading Levels:** Reading levels for all the story characters and group readings can be found in each of the fairy tales teacher's guides. Teachers can thereby assign character roles according to individual reading skills.

4. **Sound Effects Audio CD:** There are 8 to 15 sound effects for each fairy tale. The sound effects tracks are found on page 5. Easy-to-follow directions about when to play each sound effect can be found in each script. This is a fun task to assign to an individual student.

5. **Simple or Elaborate Productions:** Every fairy tale can become an elaborate production when you incorporate the ideas found under "Optional Costume & Set Suggestions" in each teacher's guide. The productions can also remain simple when you use the easy-to-make reproducible props found on the pages following each script.

Reader's Theater Teacher's Guide

The concept of Reader's Theater as well as the scripts, props, and other materials used in the classroom can become powerful tools that not only help children improve fluency and comprehension skills, but have also been found to enhance listening, writing, and social skills, and increase self-confidence.

Here are some tips to assist you in creating successful Readers' Theater experiences in your classroom:

1. **Review the Traditional Tale:** Every script included in Fairy Tale Readers' Theater is a traditional and well-loved tale. Before introducing the script, review the original fairy tale with your students. A list of literature resources is provided under "Review the Traditional Story" in each teacher's guide.

2. **Teach New Vocabulary:** A list of the new and more difficult words are included in each teacher's guide under "Teach New Vocabulary." It is recommended that these words are taught and then reviewed before reading the script. The children need to be able to read and understand the meanings of the words. Write the new vocabulary words on large cards and add them to your word wall. Illustrate each new word.

3. **Highlight the Text:** The scripts were created in the font ITC Stone Informal, 14 point —an easy-to-read font for children. Have each student trace over each of their lines using a bright highlighter. This will help the reader's stay on track.

4. **First Read-Through:** The first read-through should be as non-threatening as possible. The goal is to learn the words and read through the text. As the children become more comfortable with the text, you can begin to encourage them to read with more dramatic expressions. Talk about reading the text using "character voices," such as cackling like a witch, or using a big, deep voice for a giant. This adds fun, a bit of drama, and increases fluency.

5. **Brainstorm Ideas for Scenery:** Costume suggestions and prop patterns are included. Have the children brainstorm ideas for scenery. Painting murals and drawing scenery on chalkboards with colored chalk is easy and can be effective. Children can be very creative and innovative.

Story Sound Effects — Audio CD Tracks

The Three Bears
CD TRACK 1:........(MUSIC TO BEGIN THE STORY)
CD TRACK 2:........(COOKING SOUNDS; STIRRING)
CD TRACK 3:........(DOOR OPENS AND THEN CLOSES)
CD TRACK 4:........(DOOR OPENS AND THEN SLAMS SHUT)
CD TRACK 5:........(BIRDS; FOREST SOUNDS)
CD TRACK 6:........(FOOTSTEPS WALKING UPSTAIRS)
CD TRACK 7:........(FOOTSTEPS RUNNING DOWN THE STAIRS AND
                    OUT THE DOOR)
CD TRACK 8:........(MUSIC TO END THE STORY)

Beauty and the Beast
CD TRACK 9:........(MUSIC TO BEGIN THE STORY)
CD TRACK 10:.......(WIND SOUNDS)
CD TRACK 11:.......(BIG "BEAST" FOOTSTEPS)
CD TRACK 12:.......(WIND SOUNDS)
CD TRACK 13:.......(WIND SOUNDS)
CD TRACK 14:.......(WIND SOUNDS)
CD TRACK 15:.......(SCARY MUSIC)
CD TRACK 16:.......(WOMAN CRYING)
CD TRACK 17:.......(WIND SOUNDS)
CD TRACK 18:.......(WEDDING MUSIC)
CD TRACK 19:.......(WIND SOUNDS)

Aladdin and His Magic Lamp
CD TRACK 20:.......(MUSIC TO BEGIN THE STORY)
CD TRACK 21:.......(DOOR OPENS, THEN SLAMS SHUT)
CD TRACK 22:.......(FOOTSTEPS RUNNING)
CD TRACK 23:.......(LOUD SWOOSH AND BANG, GENIE APPEARS)
CD TRACK 24:.......(KNOCKING AT DOOR)
CD TRACK 25:.......(FOOTSTEPS, DOOR OPENS AND THEN SHUTS)
CD TRACK 26:.......(LOUD SWOOSH AND BANG, GENIE APPEARS)
CD TRACK 27:.......(LOUD SWOOSH AND BANG, GENIE DISAPPEARS)
CD TRACK 28:.......(LOUD SWOOSH AND BANG, GENIE APPEARS)
CD TRACK 29:.......(LOUD SWOOSH AND BANG, GENIE DISAPPEARS)
CD TRACK 30:.......(KNOCKING AT DOOR)

Jack and the Beanstalk
CD TRACK 31:.......(MUSIC TO BEGIN THE STORY)
CD TRACK 32:.......(COW MOOING)
CD TRACK 33:.......(BEANS FALLING OUT)
CD TRACK 34:.......(MOTHER CRYING)
CD TRACK 35:.......(LOUD KNOCKING, HUGE DOOR OPENS)
CD TRACK 36:.......(FOOTSTEPS RUNNING, BUMPS INTO GIANT'S WIFE)
CD TRACK 37:.......(HUGE DOOR SHUTS)
CD TRACK 38:.......(LOUD KNOCKING, HUGE DOOR OPENS)
CD TRACK 39:.......(FOOTSTEPS RUNNING, BUMPS INTO GIANT'S WIFE)
CD TRACK 40:.......(HEN CLUCKING)
CD TRACK 41:.......(LOUD KNOCKING, HUGE DOOR OPENS)
CD TRACK 42:.......(FOOTSTEPS RUNNING, BUMPS INTO GIANT'S WIFE)
CD TRACK 43:.......(GIANT'S HUGE FOOTSTEPS)
CD TRACK 44:.......(HARP MUSIC)

Hansel and Gretel
CD TRACK 45:.......(MUSIC TO BEGIN THE STORY)
CD TRACK 46:.......(FOREST SOUNDS)
CD TRACK 47:.......(FOREST SOUNDS)
CD TRACK 48:.......(FOREST SOUNDS)
CD TRACK 49:.......(MANY BIRDS CHIRPING)
CD TRACK 50:.......(FOREST SOUNDS)

CD TRACK 51:......(DOOR OPENS, THEN CLOSES)
CD TRACK 52:......(DOOR SLAMS SHUT, BOY SCREAMS)
CD TRACK 53:......(SNORING)
CD TRACK 54:......(FOREST SOUNDS)
CD TRACK 55:......(FOREST SOUNDS)

Pied Piper of Hamelin
CD TRACK 56:......(MUSIC TO BEGIN THE STORY)
CD TRACK 57:......(ANGRY CROWD SOUNDS)
CD TRACK 58:......(ANGRY CROWD SOUNDS)
CD TRACK 59:......(KNOCKING ON DOOR)
CD TRACK 60:......(FLUTE MUSIC)
CD TRACK 61:......(CROWD CHEERING)
CD TRACK 62:......(DOOR SLAMS SHUT)
CD TRACK 63:......(CROWD TALKING)
CD TRACK 64:......(ANGRY CROWD SOUNDS)
CD TRACK 65:......(ANGRY CROWD SOUNDS)

Little Red Riding Hood
CD TRACK 66:......(MUSIC TO BEGIN THE STORY)
CD TRACK 67:......(DOOR OPENS, THEN CLOSES)
CD TRACK 68:......(FOREST SOUNDS)
CD TRACK 69:......(KNOCKING ON DOOR)
CD TRACK 70:......(KNOCKING ON DOOR)
CD TRACK 71:......(EVIL MUSIC)
CD TRACK 72:......(CRASHING SOUND)
CD TRACK 73:......(STRUGGLING/FIGHTING SOUNDS)

Elves and the Shoemaker
CD TRACK 74:......(MUSIC TO BEGIN THE STORY)
CD TRACK 75:......(CREAKING WINDOW OPENS, THEN CLOSES)
CD TRACK 76:......(HAMMERING SOUNDS)
CD TRACK 77:......(CASH REGISTER)
CD TRACK 78:......(HAMMERING SOUNDS)
CD TRACK 79:......(HAMMERING SOUNDS)
CD TRACK 80:......(CREAKING WINDOW OPENS, THEN CLOSES)

Cinderella
CD TRACK 81:......(MUSIC TO BEGIN THE STORY)
CD TRACK 82:......(HORSE AND CARRIAGE SOUNDS)
CD TRACK 83:......(FLASH AND BOOM, FAIRY GODMOTHER APPEARS)
CD TRACK 84:......(HORSE AND CARRIAGE SOUNDS)
CD TRACK 85:......(FOOTSTEPS RUNNING)
CD TRACK 86:......(HORSE AND CARRIAGE SOUNDS)

Snow White and the Seven Dwarfs
CD TRACK 87:......(MUSIC TO BEGIN THE STORY)
CD TRACK 88:......(KNOCKING AT DOOR)
CD TRACK 89:......(DOOR OPENS, THEN CLOSES)
CD TRACK 90:......(FALLING TO THE FLOOR)
CD TRACK 91:......(DOOR OPENS, THEN CLOSES, FOOTSTEPS RUNNING)
CD TRACK 92:......(KNOCKING AT DOOR)
CD TRACK 93:......(DOOR OPENS. THEN CLOSES)
CD TRACK 94:......(FALLING TO THE FLOOR)
CD TRACK 95:......(MANY CRYING)
CD TRACK 96:......(KNOCKING AT DOOR)
CD TRACK 97:......(KISSING)
CD TRACK 98:......(MUSIC TO END THE STORY)

Coorelations to the Standards

This book supports the NCTE/IRA Standards for the English Language Arts and the recommended teaching practices outlined in the NAEYC/IRA position statement Learning to Read and Write: Developmentally Appropriate Practices for Young Children.

NCTE/IRA Standards for the English Language Arts

Each activity in this book supports one or more of the following standards:

1. **Students read many different types of print and nonprint texts for a variety of purposes.** *Fairy Tale Readers' Theater* contains 10 readers' theater scripts that students read to improve fluency and comprehension skills. In addition, it includes literature suggestions that students can read to learn more about the classic fairy tales upon which the scripts are based.

2. **Students read literature from various time periods, cultures, and genres in order to form an understanding of humanity.** The scripts in *Fairy Tale Readers' Theater* are based on classic fairy tales from various times and cultures, and the literature suggestions include different tellings of these tales, so students learn about different perspectives on the same story by doing the activities in this book.

3. **Students use a variety of strategies to build meaning while reading.** The repeated reading of the scripts in this book, along with specific fluency activities, build fluency skills that aid in comprehension. In addition, enrichment activities in each chapter support such skills and strategies as vocabulary development, drawing conclusions, inferring, reading for details, and comparing and contrasting.

4. **Students communicate in spoken, written, and visual form, for a variety of purposes and a variety of audiences.** Students communicate in all three of these forms throughout the activities in *Fairy Tale Readers' Theater*. They communicate in spoken form while performing the scripts and participating in classroom discussion, they write things such as lists, descriptions, and notes, and they communicate visually through drawing and by helping to create props and costumes for the scripts.

5. **Students become participating members of a variety of literacy communities.** Because Readers' Theater is inherently a group activity, doing the activities in this book is a very effective way to build a classroom literacy community.

NAEYC/IRA Position Statement Learning to Read and Write: Developmentally Appropriate Practices for Young Children

Each activity in this book supports one or more of the following recommended teaching practices for Kindergarten and Primary students:

1. **Teachers read to children daily and provide opportunities for students to independently read both fiction and nonfiction texts.** *Fairy Tale Readers' Theater* includes 10 Readers' Theater scripts that students read aloud along with literature suggestions that teachers can read to students or students can read independently.

2. **Teachers provide opportunities for students to write many different kinds of texts for different purposes.** The enrichment activities in *Fairy Tale Readers' Theater* include writing activities such as lists, notes, and descriptions.

3. **Teachers provide challenging instruction that expands children's knowledge of their world and expands vocabulary.** The scripts in *Fairy Tale Readers' Theater*, based on classic fairy tales, introduce children to well-loved literature. In addition, each chapter includes a vocabulary list to expand students' vocabulary.

4. **Teachers adapt teaching strategies based on the individual needs of a child.** The varying reading levels in the scripts in *Fairy Tale Readers' Theater* allow teachers to assign students parts that fit their individual needs.

The Three Bears

PERFORMANCE PREPARATION SCRIPT AND PROPS

Characters and Reading Levels

The Three Bears includes 6 characters and a group choral reading.

- Dad Bear .... reading level 2.2
- Mom Bear .... reading level 2.5
- Teenage Bear.............. reading level 2.6
- Goldilocks.................. reading level 2.7
- Goldilock's Mom .... reading level 1.9
- Narrator .... reading level 2.1
- Forest (group)............. reading level 1.7

The "Forest" choral reading can be read by a small or a large group—allowing the entire class to participate. You may also choose to eliminate the choral reading. Make a single copy of the script and "white-out" the lines of the "Forest." Then, copy the edited script for the 6 performing story characters.

Reproducible Script and Props

- Reproduce the script: *The Three Bears,* found on pages 8–11 for each student.
- Make the story props—patterns and directions are found on pages 11–14.

Audio CD Sound Effects

- Sound effects for *The Three Bears,* are found on tracks 1–8. Directions for when to play each sound effect can be found in the script.

Optional Costume & Set Suggestions

- Bears' ears: Use bear ear patterns (page 11) and cut them out of brown felt. Glue pink felt circles inside the ears. Glue to headbands.
- Teenage Bear: baseball cap and shirt
- Mom Bear: apron
- Dad Bear: hat, bow tie, draw whiskers with an eyebrow pencil
- Goldilocks: braid yellow yarn and attach to a headband.

READING PREPARATION AND ENRICHMENT ACTIVITIES

Review the Traditional Story

- *The Three Bears* by Byron Barton. HarperCollins (1991)
- *Goldilocks and the Three Bears* by Valeri Gorbachev. North-South Books (2003)
- *Goldilocks and the Three Bears* by James Marshall. Puffin Picture Books (1998)
- *Goldilocks and the Three Bears* by Jan Brett. Putnam Juvenile (1996)
- *The Three Snow Bears* by Jan Brett Putnam. Juvenile (1972).

Teach New Vocabulary

Teach the following vocabulary (word recognition and meaning) prior to reading the script: *breakfast, broke, empty, forest, Goldilocks, hungry, moan, narrator, ouch, person, police, porridge, teenage, tiptoe, whispers.*

Encourage Fluency

- First, read through the script without using any of the props.
- Teach the children that words that are printed in all capital letters should be spoken with special emphasis, such as "Someone broke MY chair."
- The Forest group reading should sound like a warning. Practice "No one is home at the Bears' house." And "Someone is home at the Bears' house." Stress the words "No one" and "someone."

Enrichment Activities

- Print the sentences (below) on large paper strips, cut apart the words, and put the words in an envelop. Have the children sequence the words into sentences and glue them in order. Then, have the children sequence the sentences according to the events of the story.
1. The Bears go for a walk.
2. Goldilocks goes into the Bears' house.
3. The Bears find Goldilocks asleep.
4. Goldilocks wakes up and runs home.

Script: The Three Bears

SCENE 1: *(In the Bears' cottage.)*

CD TRACK 1: . *(MUSIC TO BEGIN THE STORY)*

Teenage Bear: .I'm hungry and I'm tired.

Mom Bear: ......If you had eaten your dinner last night you wouldn't be hungry.

Dad Bear: ....If you had gone to bed when we told you, you wouldn't be tired.

Teenage Bear: .Why do you always moan at me?

Mom Bear: ......*(sighing)* If you did what we asked, we wouldn't have to.

Dad Bear: ....And, if you did what we asked, you wouldn't be tired and hungry.

Narrator: ....Mom Bear is making porridge for breakfast.

CD TRACK 2: .... *(COOKING SOUNDS; STIRRING)*

Teenage Bear: .*(eats some porridge)* Ouch! This is too hot. You know I don't like it hot!

Mom Bear: ......I've had it! I'm going for a walk!

Dad Bear: ....Good idea. Let's all go. A walk will calm us down. Then, we can come back and have a nice breakfast.

Mom Bear: ......What do you say, son? Let's try and get along.

Teenage Bear: .*(in grumpy voice)* If I have to.

Narrator: ....The Bears leave the house and go for a walk.

CD TRACK 3: .... *(DOOR OPENS AND THEN CLOSES)*

Forest (group): No one is home at the Bears' house.

SCENE 2: *(Goldilocks at home with her Mom.)*

Narrator: ....Goldilocks is at home. Her Mom is making her breakfast.

Goldilocks: ......Not this again! I hate fried eggs!

Goldilock's Mom: ...Don't talk to me like that! You should just say thank you.

Goldilocks: ......I'm sick of it here.

Narrator: ....Goldilocks gets up and goes to the door.

Goldilock's Mom: ...Where do you think you're going?

Goldilocks: ......Anywhere is better than here!

Goldilock's Mom: ...You think you can just walk out the door?

Goldilocks: ......Easy!

Goldilock's Mom: ...We'll see young lady. You had better not go too far away!

   CD TRACK 4: .... *(DOOR OPENS AND THEN SLAMS SHUT)*

Forest (group): No one is home at the Bears' house.

SCENE 3: *(Goldilocks walks in the woods, and sees the Bears' house)*

Narrator: ....Goldilocks is walking through the woods. She sees the Bears' house.

   CD TRACK 5: .... *(BIRDS; FOREST SOUNDS)*

Goldilocks: .....*(to herself)* Look at that cute house. The door's open.

Narrator: ....Goldilocks opens the door and goes inside the house.

Goldilocks: .....Oh look! Porridge! *(she eats from Teenage Bear's bowl)* Yummm! This is better than Mom's fried eggs.

Forest (group): No one is home at the Bears' house.

SCENE 4: *(Back at the Bears' home)*

Narrator: ....The Bear family has come back home.

Dad Bear: ....Son, wasn't that a nice walk?

Teenage Bear: .I guess — if you like trees — which I don't.

Mom Bear:.......Come on! No more arguing.

Narrator: ....The Bears go into the kitchen. They see that someone has been in their house!

Mom Bear:.......Oh no! Look! Someone came in and broke a chair.

Teenage Bear: .Someone broke MY chair. It's not fair!

Dad Bear: ....And look! Someone ate our food!

Teenage Bear: .Not OUR food—MY food! MY bowl's empty. It's not fair!

Forest (group): Someone else is home at the Bears' house.

Mom Bear:........*(whispers)* What if the person is still in the house?

Dad Bear: ....*(whispers)* Let's look upstairs.

    CD TRACK 6:........ *(FOOTSTEPS WALKING UPSTAIRS)*

Narrator: ....They all tiptoe upstairs. They find Goldilocks asleep.

Mom Bear:........*(whispers)* It's a girl.

Dad Bear: ....*(whispers)* She's sleeping.

Teenage Bear: .*(shouts)* In my bed! Who does she think she is?

Goldilocks: ....*(waking up)* Bears! Help! Save me! Bears!

Teenage Bear: .Help? Save me? You broke MY chair! You ate MY food! You slept in MY bed! Why are you yelling?

Goldilocks: ......Bears are mean! Don't bears eat people?

Teenage Bear: .I don't. I eat Porridge—unless someone else eats it first.

Mom Bear:.......This is our home. You can't just help yourself to our things?

Dad Bear: ....We should call the police.

Goldilocks: ......Please don't. My Mom will be so mad!

Teenage Bear: .My Mom and Dad work hard to make this a nice house.

Goldilocks: ......I'm really sorry.

Teenage Bear: .And, she always cooks good food.

Goldilocks: ......Oh, it did taste good.

Teenage Bear: .You just take, take, and take, don't you?

Goldilocks: ......You are right. I do! I'm the same way with my Mom, I have been so selfish. I'm sorry. I must go and tell my mom that I'm sorry.

Forest (group): Goldilocks should leave the Bears' house.

Narrator: ....Goldilocks gets up and looks at Mom and Dad Bear.

Goldilocks: ......You have a good son. I will try to be more like him.

Narrator: ....Goldilocks leaves and waves goodbye.

    CD TRACK 7:........ *(FOOTSTEPS RUNNING DOWN THE STAIRS AND OUT THE DOOR)*

Dad Bear: ....Well, well, well!

Mom Bear:.......*(teasing)* Did you hear that? She will try to be more like you.

Teenage Son:...*(laughing)* Ok, Ok. I 'm sorry.

Narrator:.........The Bears all hug each other.

Mom Bear:.......Anyone hungry? Someone should make breakfast.

Dad Bear: ....Mmm, I wonder who should cook?

Narrator: ....The Bears both look at their son.

Teenage Bear: .Ok. Ok. I'll try. But, I don't think I am a very good cook.

Mom Bear:.......*(laughs)* Come on. We will all help. It's more fun that way.

Forest (group): Everything is good at the Bears' house.

  CD TRACK 8: .*(MUSIC TO END THE STORY)*

  THE END

The Three Bears Prop Patterns

Directions: Copy, color, cut out, and laminate for durability. Tape to a plastic headband.

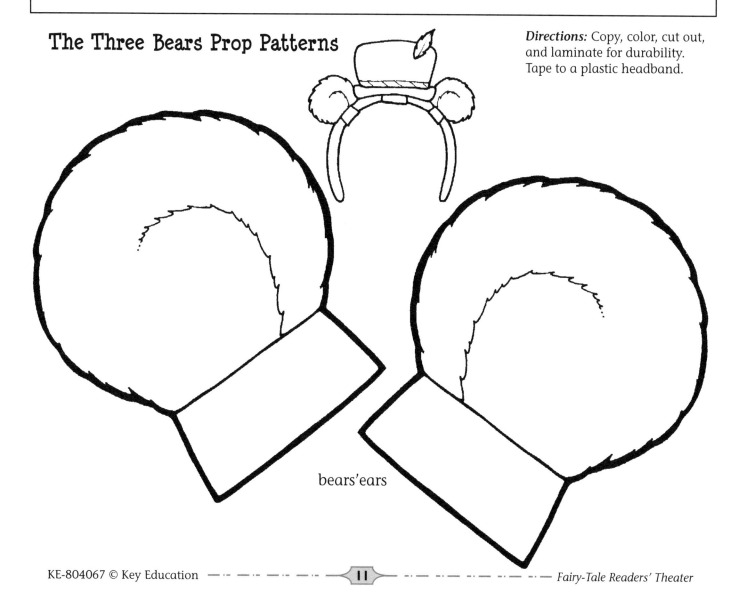

bears'ears

The Three Bears Prop Patterns

Directions: Copy, color, cut out, and laminate for durability. Tape to a plastic headbpand.

Dad Bear's hat

Mom Bear's bow

Teenage Bear's cap

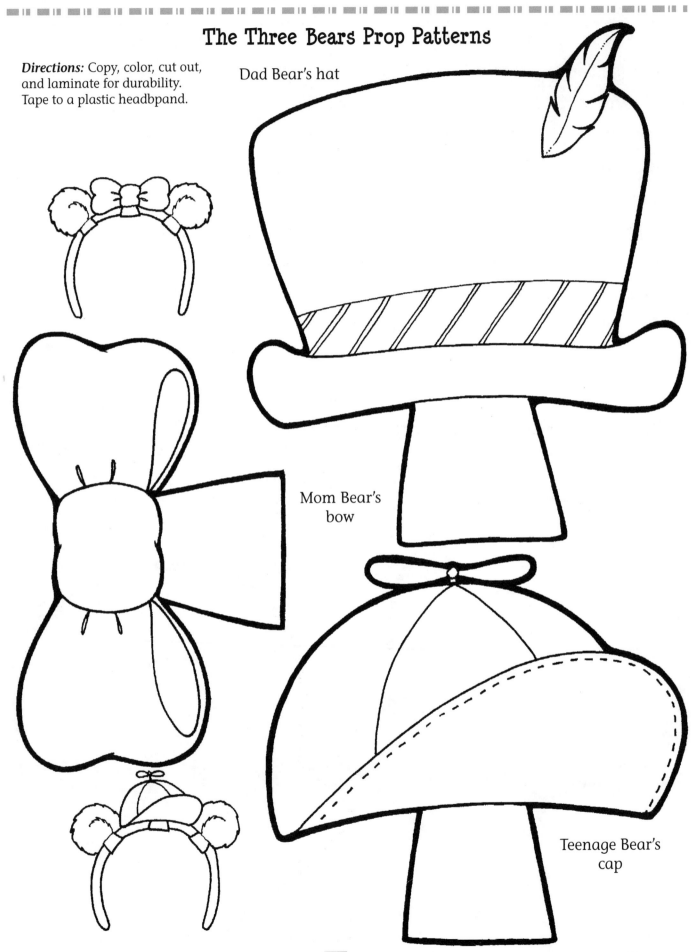

Goldilock's pigtails

Directions: Copy, color, cut out, and laminate for durability. Tape to a plastic headband.

Dad Bear

Dad Bear's porridge

Directions: Copy, color, cut out, and laminate for durability.

Mom Bear's porridge

Directions: Copy, color, cut out, and laminate for durability.

Mom Bear

TEENAGE BEAR

Teenage Bear's porridge

Beauty and The Beast

PERFORMANCE PREPARATION SCRIPT AND PROPS

Characters and Reading Levels

Beauty and The Beast includes six characters and a group choral reading.

- Beauty .... reading level 2.4
- Beauty's Dad .... reading level 2.1
- Blossom (sister) .... reading level 2.8
- Daisy (sister).............. reading level 2.5
- Beast.......................... reading level 2.8
- Narrator .... reading level 2.7
- Wind (group) .... reading level 2.3

The "Wind" choral reading can be read by a small or a large group—allowing the entire class to participate. You may also choose to eliminate the choral reading. Make a single copy of the script and "white-out" the lines of the "Wind." Then, copy the edited script for the 6 performing story characters.

Reproducible Script and Props

- Reproduce the script: *Beauty and The Beast,* found on pages 16–19 for each student.
- Make the story props—patterns and directions are found on pages 20–22.

Audio CD Sound Effects

- Sound effects for *Beauty and The Beast,* are found on tracks 9–19. Directions for when to play each sound effect can be found in the script.

Optional Costume & Set Suggestions

- Beast: Copy pattern (page 21) onto card stock. Cut apart gray, brown, and black yarn and glue onto mask to represent fur. Add a black felt nose. Wear brown gloves for paws, a suit jacket, and red scarf tied around waist.
- Beauty and sisters: simple long dresses
- Beauty's Dad: jacket; add gray eyebrows and wrinkles with gray eyebrow pencil.
- Castle: Make a mural of a large castle with tress to use as the background.

READING PREPARATION AND ENRICHMENT ACTIVITIES

Review the Traditional Story

- *Beauty and the Beast* by Marianna Mayer and Mercer Mayer. Chronicle Books (2002)
- *Beauty and the Beast* by Max Eilenberg and Angela Barrett. Walker Books Ltd (2006)
- *Beauty: A Retelling of the Story of Beauty and the Beast* by Robin Mckinley. Eos (2005)
- *Beauty and the Beast* (Read-Aloud Board Book) by RH Disney. Disney (2004)

Teach New Vocabulary

Teach the following vocabulary (word recognition and meaning) prior to reading the script: *Beauty, Beast, Blossom, candles, castle, darling, Daisy, daughters, handsome, hurry, marry, minutes, narrator, prince, promise, scary, strong, ugly.*

Encourage Fluency

- First, read through the script without using any of the props.
- The lines for the "wind" are written as short poems. The text has a rhythm that helps the students read smoothly.
- Ask the students to try and make their voices sound like the wind by stretching the last word in each sentence. For example, "Beauty must goooo. She can't say nooooo."

Enrichment Activities

- Drawing conclusions: Ask the students why they think the prince had a spell cast on him.
- Inferences: Discuss the ending of the story. Why did the wind say, "If the prince loves her, he'd better grow some fur!"?
- The Five W's: Ask the children who, what, when, where, and why questions about the story.

Script: Beauty and the Beast

SCENE 1: *(Beauty's Home)*

CD TRACK 9: .... *(MUSIC TO BEGIN THE STORY)*

Beauty's Father: ... Are you sure you don't mind going?

Beauty: .... I can save your life if I go and live with the Beast. I have to go!

Daisy: .... If you hadn't asked Dad to bring you a rose. We wouldn't be in this mess.

Blossom: .... Dad, is the Beast really scary?

Beauty's Father: ... He looks scary. But he was very kind. He gave me food and drink. He also gave me nice things to bring home to you.

Daisy: .... It's not kind to say "give me one of your daughters or I'll kill you!"

Beauty's Father: ... I know, but I think he really is a kind Beast.

Beauty: .... Let's hope you're right, Dad.

CD TRACK 10: ...... *(WIND SOUNDS)*

Wind (group): ...... Beauty must go. She can't say "no."

SCENE 2: *(In the Beast's Palace.)*

Narrator: .... Beauty is at the Beast's castle. She has been alone all day. The Beast is coming to eat dinner with her. There are two places set at the table. She hears him coming.

Beauty: .... *(to herself)* Be brave, be brave, be brave.

CD TRACK 11: ..... *(BIG "BEAST" FOOTSTEPS)*

Narrator: .... The Beast comes in. He's big and furry, with a huge nose and pointed teeth.

Beast: .... Hello, Beauty. I hope you like it here.

Beauty: .... I do. Thank you. Your home is very nice. I love candles.

Beast: .... Thank you. Let's eat.

Narrator:	Beauty and the Beast enjoyed their meal. They talked and talked.
Beast:	Did you like your food?
Beauty:	It was the best food I have ever eaten.
Beast:	Did you enjoy talking to me?
Beauty:	I did.
Beast:	Then, will you marry me?
Beauty:	No, I'm sorry. I can't marry you.
Beast:	Good night, Beauty.
Narrator:	The Beast gets up and leaves the room. He looks very sad.
Beauty:	Marry him? I've only known him five minutes. But, he is kind of cute. He is also very nice.
CD TRACK 12:	*(WIND SOUNDS)*
Wind (group):	The Beast was feeling blue. Beauty said, "I can't marry you."

SCENE 3: *(Beauty's home)*

Narrator:	Beauty has lived with the Beast for a while. He let her go home to visit her family. She promised she would return in three days.
Blossom:	Is he awful?
Daisy:	Is he ugly?
Beauty's Father:	Is he kind?
Beauty:	Yes, he's kind. He's big and strong. He loves to talk. He has lots of fur.
Blossom/Daisy	Fur!
Beauty:	Yes, but it's very soft and very clean!
Blossom:	What do you talk about?
Beauty:	Music, books, all kinds of things. And every day he asks me to marry him.
Daisy:	Gross!
Blossom:	Ick!
Beauty:	Not really. He's always very nice when I tell him "no."

Beauty's Father:... And, he let you come and visit! Oh, Beauty! It's so good to see you. How long can you stay?

Beauty: .... Only three days. Then, I must go back. I promised him.

CD TRACK 13: ..... *(WIND SOUNDS)*

Wind (group): ...... Beauty went to see her Dad. She left the Beast very sad.

SCENE 4: *(Beauty's is still at home)*

Narrator: .... It has been four days. Beauty has to get back to the Beast.

Beauty's Father:... Please stay one more day.

Daisy: .... You just got here.

Blossom: .... He won't mind one more day.

Beauty: .... Don't make this hard for me. I must go. He said I had to be back in three days. I'm a day late. I have to go now.

Daisy: .... You want to go back to him?

Blossom: .... Do you love him?

Beauty: .... How could I? He's a beast! But, I made a promise.

Beauty's Father:... She's right girls. We must let her go. Please, come back soon.

Beauty: .... I'll try.

CD TRACK 14: ..... *(WIND SOUNDS)*

Wind (group): ...... Beauty is late. Hurry! Don't wait!

SCENE 5: *(The Beast's Palace)*

Narrator: .... Beauty arrives back at the Beast's castle. She finds him lying on the floor.

CD TRACK 15: ..... *(SCARY MUSIC)*

Beauty: .... Oh no! Is he dead? He is! He's dead! If I'd come back on time he'd still be alive. Why didn't I tell him I loved him? Now, it's too late.

CD TRACK 16: ..... *(WOMAN CRYING)*

Narrator: .... When Beauty cries, her tears fall on the Beast's face. The tears turn him into a handsome prince.

Beast: .... *(opens his eyes)* I knew you'd save me.

Beauty: ....What? Where's the Beast gone? Who are you? You're all smooth! You're not furry.

Beast: ....This is the real me! A spell was cast on me. It made me ugly until I found someone who could love me.

Beauty: ....Oh! What a surprise!

Beast: ....Will you marry me now?

Beauty: ....Errrr, yes, of course I will.

    CD TRACK 17: .....*(WIND SOUNDS)*

Wind (group): ......What a surprise! Wow! Will they marry now?

<u>SCENE 6</u>: *(At the Palace after the wedding)*

    CD TRACK 18: .....*(WEDDING MUSIC)*

Blossom: ....It's not fair.

Daisy: ....All the good things happen to her.

Blossom: ....She gets the palace and the Prince!

Daisy: ....And what a Prince! He's a dream.

Blossom: ....You'd think Beauty would be happy.

Daisy: ....I know! She's looked sad all day.

Prince: ....You look beautiful, Beauty!

Beauty: ....Thanks. So, do you.

Prince: ....I do, don't I? I'm so happy to be handsome again! *(Looks in mirror)*

Beauty: ....Darling?

Prince: ....Yes, Darling?

Beauty: ....Oh, nothing.

Prince: ....What is it? Tell me.

Beauty: ....Have you ever thought of growing a beard?

    CD TRACK 19: .....*(WIND SOUNDS)*

Wind (group): ......If the Prince loves her—he better grow some fur!

THE END

Beauty and the Beast Prop Patterns

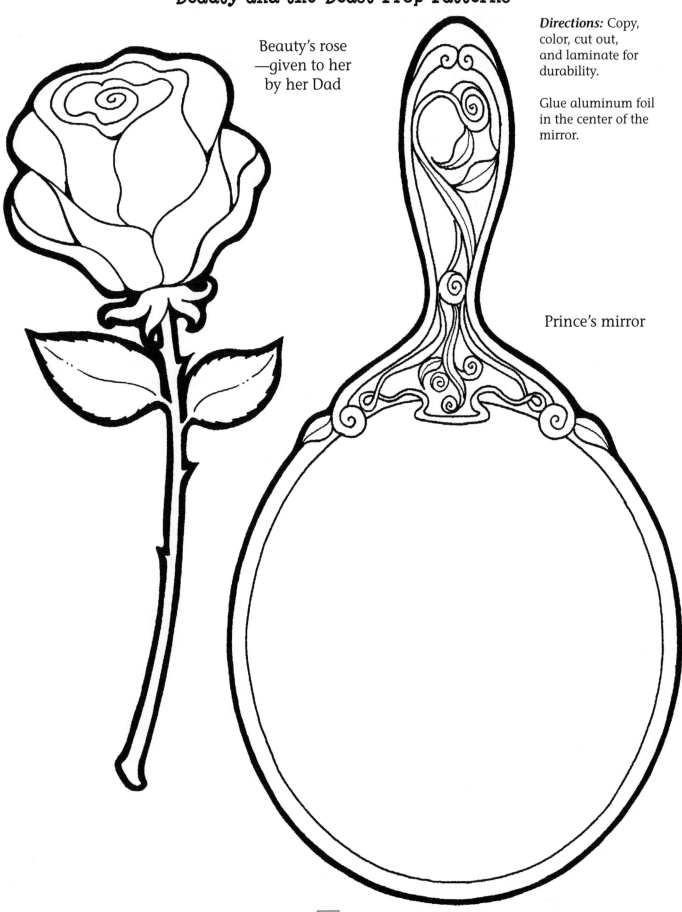

Beauty's rose
—given to her
by her Dad

Directions: Copy,
color, cut out,
and laminate for
durability.

Glue aluminum foil
in the center of the
mirror.

Prince's mirror

Beauty and the Beast
Prop Patterns

Beast mask

(cut out)   (cut out)

Directions: Copy, color, cut out, and laminate for durability.

Cut out eye holes. Tape a construction paper strip from the left side to the right side of the mask so that it fits the child's head comfortably.

Beauty and the Beast Prop Patterns

Directions: Copy, color, cut out, and laminate for durability. Tape a toilet paper cardboard tube on the back so the candelabra so it can stand up.

candelabra

Prince's crown

Directions: Copy, color, cut out and laminate for durability. Glue on sequins and plastic "jewels." Tape to a plastic headband or staple a construction paper strip so that it fits the child's head.

Aladdin & His Magic Lamp

PERFORMANCE PREPARATION SCRIPT AND PROPS

Characters and Reading Levels

Aladdin & His Magic Lamp includes six characters and a group choral reading.

- Aladdin .... reading level 2.5
- Widow Twanky (Aladdin's mother) ..... reading level 2.2
- Jasmine .... reading level 2.1
- Sultan .... reading level 2.3
- Genie .... reading level 2.2
- Narrator .... reading level 2.2
- Crowd (group) .... reading level 1.3

The "Crowd" choral reading can be read by a small or a large group—allowing the entire class to participate. You may also choose to eliminate the choral reading. Make a single copy of the script and "white-out" the lines of the "Crowd." Then, copy the edited script for the 6 performing story characters.

Reproducible Script and Props

- Reproduce the script: *Aladdin & His Magic Lamp,* found on pages 24–29 for each student.
- Make the story props—patterns and directions are found on pages 29–32.

Audio CD Sound Effects

- Sound effects for *Aladdin & His Magic Lamp,* are found on tracks 20–30. Directions for when to play each sound effect can be found in the script.

Optional Costume & Set Suggestions

- Aladdin and Sultan: colorful scarves wrapped around their heads as turbans.
- Jasmine: Scarf over head with a head band across the forehead; long dress.
- Widow Twanky: Dark colored dress; dark scarf draped over her head.
- Genie: Colorful shirt and baggy pants; scarf wrapped around head.
- Use a real oil lamp.

READING PREPARATION AND ENRICHMENT ACTIVITIES

Review the Traditional Story

- *Aladdin and Other Tales from the Arabian Nights* by Anonymous, William Harvey, and N. J. Dawood. Puffin. (1997)
- *Aladdin And The Enchanted Lamp* by Philip Pullman and Sophy Williams. Arthur A. Levine Books (2005)
- *Aladdin* by Golden Books. (1989)
- *Aladdin & His Magical Lamp* by Katie Daynes and Paddy Mounter. Usborne Books (2003)
- *Aladdin and Other Favorite Arabian Nights Stories* by Philip Smith. Dover Publications (1993)

Teach New Vocabulary

Teach the following vocabulary (word recognition and meaning) prior to reading the script: *Aladdin, command, crowd, daughter, Genie, granted, guards, husband, Jasmine, lazy, magic, master, mistake, palace, prince, princess, rude, Sultan, Widow Twanky.*

Encourage Fluency

- First, read through the script without using any of the props.
- The "Crowd" has the same line throughout the entire script which is great for struggling readers. The line is, "OH, WOW! What will happen now?" Explain how "OH, WOW!" should be exclaimed and the rest of the sentence should be said with as a big question.
- There is a lot of emotion in this story. Practice saying the same sentence in different emotions. For example, say the sentence, "I want to go to a movie." Say it using happy, sad, angry, and excited expressions.

Enrichment Activities

- If you were granted tree wishes, what would they be?
- Draw a picture of what you think it looks like inside of the Gennie's lamp.

Script: Aladdin and His Magic Lamp

SCENE 1: *(Aladdin's home)*

CD TRACK 20:..... *(MUSIC TO BEGIN THE STORY)*

CD TRACK 21:..... *(DOOR OPENS, THEN SLAMS SHUT)*

Widow Twanky:..Where have you been, you lazy boy?

Aladdin:...............Locked in a magic cave!

Widow Twanky:..Of course you have. And, I've just been to the moon.

Aladdin:...............It's true! I rubbed my magic ring and a genie came out. He let me out of the cave.

Widow Twanky:..Oh really! Can your genie find you a job? Can he stop you from being so lazy?

Aladdin:...............Go ahead and make fun of me. It's true. Look, this is the lamp the magician gave me. It's proof.

Widow Twanky:..It's not proof – it's a piece of junk. I don't want it. Now, go and find a job. We need money or we can't eat.

Crowd: ....OH, WOW! What will happen now?

SCENE 2: *(Sultan's Palace)*

Narrator:...............Jasmine and her father, the Sultan, are at the palace. They are arguing.

Jasmine: ....I've told you! I will marry for love. And I will choose the man.

Sultan: ....Where do you get these crazy ideas? I am your father. I will choose your husband.

Jasmine:...............I will never, ever marry unless it is for love.

Sultan: ....I will have to lock you up until you change your mind. I am doing this for your own good.

Jasmine:...............You'll have to catch me first.

Narrator: ....Jasmine runs out of the palace.

CD TRACK 22:.....*(FOOTSTEPS RUNNING)*

Sultan: ....Guards! Guards! Go and find the Princess.

Crowd: ....OH, WOW! What will happen now?

SCENE 3: *(Aladdin's home)*

Aladdin:...............Mom! Mom! Guess who I just met?

Widow Twanky:..Let me guess, Brad Pitt? Madonna? The Sultan?

Aladdin:...............Close! The Sultan's daughter.

Widow Twanky:..I should have guessed. Don't tell me. You fell in love and she wants to marry you.

Aladdin:...............Yes! How did you know?

Widow Twanky:..You and your lies! You lie so much—you think you're telling the truth.

Aladdin:...............But I am! She ran away from the Palace. The Sultan wants her to marry this old man who works for him. We met at the market, and… we fell in love.

Widow Twanky:..You have gone crazy. Even if it was true, you can't marry her. You're not a prince. The Princess can only marry a prince.

Aladdin:...............I know. It's not fair. What can we do?

Widow Twanky:..*(picks lamp off shelf)* I'm sick of your tales. I'm off to the market. I will try and sell this piece of junk. We need the money. Clean it up for me will you? I'll be back soon.

Narrator: ....Aladdin's mother leaves the room. Aladdin rubs the lamp.

CD TRACK 23:......*(LOUD SWOOSH AND BANG, GENIE APPEARS)*

Narrator: ....There's a loud flash and a bang. A big, angry looking genie is standing in the room.

Genie:...................About time you got me out! How would you like to be kept in a tiny lamp —year after year after year?

Aladdin:...............Who are you?

Genie:...................The Genie of the lamp, silly boy — I mean Master. Who do you think I am?

Aladdin:..............Sorry, I'm just surprised! So, do I get whatever I ask for?

Genie:..................You get three wishes. You must know that. What do they teach you kids in schools these days?

Aladdin:..............Great! I wish to be a prince. Then, I can marry the Princess. Can you do that?

Genie:..................Yes, that's easy. I am the greatest Genie in the world!

Aladdin:..............Boy, did I get lucky! How can I thank you?

Genie:..................There is one tiny thing you can do for me.

Aladdin:..............Name it – it's yours.

Genie:..................Use your last wish to set me free.

Aladdin:..............All I want to do is to marry the Princess. So sure, you can have my last wish.

Genie:..................Thank you, Master. I shall make you the most handsome prince ever!

Crowd: ....OH, WOW! What will happen now?

SCENE 4: *(At the palace)*

Sultan: ....Don't you ever, ever, run away again!

Jasmine: ....I will if you make me marry a man I don't love.

Sultan: ....Keep an open mind. I've met a new prince. He's young and handsome. I am sure you will want to marry him.

Jasmine:...............He's never met me! How can he want to marry me?

Narrator: ....There is a knock at the door.

CD TRACK 24:......*(KNOCKING AT DOOR)*

Sultan: ....Here he is now!   Come in!

Narrator: ....Aladdin comes in dressed as a prince. Princess Jasmine doesn't know that it's Aladdin.

Aladdin:..............Jasmine! My bride to be!

Jasmine:...............Yea, right. We've never met!

Aladdin:...............*(whispers)* It's me!

Jasmine:.............*(whispers back)* So, what? I don't know you.

Sultan: ....Prince, I'm sorry my daughter is so rude. I'll leave you alone to get to know each other. Jasmine, be polite!

CD TRACK 25:.....*(FOOTSTEPS, DOOR OPENS AND THEN SHUTS)*

Narrator: ....The Sultan leaves the room.

Aladdin:.............. Jasmine, it's me. A genie turned me into a prince! Look. *(he takes off his big hat)*

Jasmine:...............Aladdin! It really is you!

Narrator: ....The Sultan comes back.

Sultan: ....How good to see you two getting along so well.

Jasmine:...............Yes, father, you knew best. You found me a great husband!

Sultan: ....I'm so pleased. Come. Let me hug you son-in-law.

Narrator: .... The Sultan hugs Aladdin and rubs the lamp by mistake.

CD TRACK 26:.....*(LOUD SWOOSH AND BANG, GENIE APPEARS)*

Narrator: ....There's a bang and a flash! Out comes the Genie.

Sultan: ....What's going on? Who is this?

Genie:..................I am the Genie of the Lamp. This is my kind Master. Your wish is my command. Your last wish Master. Don't forget your promise.

Aladdin:...............No, of course not.

Sultan: ....How wonderful! Not only does my daughter have a prince to marry, but he is a prince with a genie.

Aladdin:...............*(whispers to Genie)* Now, he knows I have a genie. I bet he'll want me to use my last wish for them. I wish you hadn't come out just then.

CD TRACK 27:.....*(LOUD SWOOSH AND BANG, GENIE DISAPPEARS)*

Genie:..................Noooooooooooooooooooooooooooooooo!

Narrator: ....There's a flash and a bang! Then, the Genie goes back in the lamp.

Aladdin:...............Woops!

Sultan: ....What's the matter?

Aladdin:...............I was going to set the Genie free with my last wish.

Jasmine:...............What Genie?

Sultan: ....What are you talking about?

Aladdin:...............*(to himself)* The Genie granted my wish that he hadn't come out – so he's made it as if he hadn't. Jasmine, do you trust me?

Jasmine:...............With my life.

Aladdin:...............And you Sultan?

Sultan: ....I'm letting you marry my daughter, aren't I?

Aladdin:...............See this lamp? I'm going to give it to you Jasmine. You will rub it, and a Genie will come out. He will give us three wishes. You can each make a wish. The third wish we will give to the Genie, so he can be free.

Jasmine:...............Wow!

Sultan: ....Go on Jasmine, rub it!

    CD TRACK 28:......*(LOUD SWOOSH AND BANG, GENIE APPEARS)*

Narrator:...............She rubbed it. Now the Genie is out! And he even looks happy.

Genie:...................Thank goodness. I thought I was going to be stuck in there for 300 years *(turns to Princess)*. You have three wishes, but if. . .

Aladdin:...............Don't worry, Genie. We'll give you the third wish.

Genie:...................Aladdin, you're a good man. Not as silly as you look.

Jasmine:...............Do I get to make the first wish?

Genie:...................Wish away, Pretty One.

Jasmine:...............I wish that Aladdin and I will be happy forever.

Genie:...................Your wish is granted.

Jasmine:...............Father, what do you want me to wish for you?

Sultan: ....Your mother died many years ago. I wish for a new wife.

Genie:...................Your wish is granted.

Jasmine:...............Now, Genie, I wish for you to be free.

Genie:...................Whoopee! Your wish is granted. I'm off!

    CD TRACK 29:......*(LOUD SWOOSH AND BANG, GENIE DISAPPEARS)*

Narrator:	.............In a puff of smoke, the Genie is gone.
Crowd:	.................OH, WOW! What will happen now?

SCENE 5: *(Aladdin's home)*

Widow Twanky:	..Oh, Aladdin! Stop making up stories.
Aladdin:	................I'm not making it up.
Widow Twanky:	..So, now you're a Prince. You look silly in those clothes. And, you think you are going to marry Princess Jasmine?
Aladdin:	...............Yes!
Widow Twanky:	..Next, you'll tell me the Sultan's coming here to ask me to marry him.
Aladdin:	...............You never know mother. You never know.
CD TRACK 30:	..... *(KNOCKING AT DOOR)*
Narrator:	.............There's a knock at the door. Aladdin sits down, smiling.
Aladdin:	...............Open the door, Mom? It might be for you.
Narrator:	.............Widow Twanky opens the door. There stands . . .
Crowd:	.................OH, WOW! What will happen now?

THE END

Aladdin and his Magic Lamp Prop Patterns

Directions: Copy, color, cut out and laminate for durability.

Magic ring

Directions: Copy, color, cut out, and laminate for durability.

Magic lamp

Aladdin and his Magic Lamp
Prop Patterns

Genie mask

(cut out)   (cut out)

Directions:
Copy, color,
cut out, and
laminate for
durability.

Cut out eye holes. Tape a
construction paper strip from
the left side to the right side
of the mask so that it fits the
child's head comfortably.

Aladdin and his Magic Lamp Prop Patterns

Smoke to cover Genie's face when he disappears

Directions: Copy, color, cut out, and laminate for durability. Tape a craft stick to the back of the smoke. The child who is playing the role of the Genie holds the smoke in front of his face when he disappears.

Jack and the Beanstalk

PERFORMANCE PREPARATION SCRIPT AND PROPS

Characters and Reading Levels

Jack and the Beanstalk includes five characters and a group choral reading.

- Jack............................ reading level 2.5
- Jack's Mother .... reading level 2.8
- Giant .... reading level 2.4
- Giant's Wife .... reading level 2.0
- Narrator .... reading level 2.5
- Birds (group) .... reading level 1.2

The "Birds" choral reading can be read by a small or a large group—allowing the entire class to participate. You may also choose to eliminate the choral reading. Make a single copy of the script and "white-out" the lines of the "Birds." Then, copy the edited script for the five performing story characters.

Reproducible Script and Props

- Reproduce the script: *Jack and the Beanstalk,* found on pages 34–39 for each student.
- Make the story props—patterns and directions are found on pages 39–41.

Audio CD Sound Effects

- Sound effects for *Jack and the Beanstalk,* are found on tracks 31–44. Directions for when to play each sound effect can be found in the script.

Optional Costume & Set Suggestions:

- Daisy, the cow: Make Daisy out of a large box; use shoe boxes as legs and for the head. A standing cow cut out would also work.
- Beanstalk: Paint several boxes green and stack them. Glue on green construction paper leaves.
- Giants: Actors stand on chairs. Using poster board, paint the giant's legs and stand them in front of the chairs. Cut the space between the giant's legs so Jack can actually crawl through them.

READING PREPARATION AND ENRICHMENT ACTIVITIES

Review the Traditional Story

- *Jack and the Beanstalk* by Steven Kellogg. HarperTrophy (1997)
- *Jack and the Beanstalk* by Carol Otto-lenghi. Brighter Child (2001)
- *Jack And the Beanstalk* by Richard Walker and Niamh Sharkey. Barefoot Books (2006)
- *Jack and the Beanstalk* (Classic Fairy Tale Collection) by John Cech and Robert Mackenzie. Sterling (2008)
- *Jack and the Beanstalk* by Paul Galdone. Clarion Books (1982)

Teach New Vocabulary

Teach the following vocabulary (word recognition and meaning) prior to reading the script: *beanstalk, blood, bored, castle, crazy, Englishman, giant, golden, greedy, grind, harp, horrid, human, proud, quick, tricked.*

Encourage Fluency

- First, read through the script without using any of the props.
- Question marks: Discuss and model how voices raise when a question is being asked. Practice with some questions from the script such as, "What is it?" "Don't you see?" "Castles in the sky?" "What?' "Where will I work?" etc.
- Giants' voices: Discuss how Giants would talk—using big, deep voices. Together, have the class say the Giant's famous line, "Fee Fi Fo Fum, I smell the blood of an Englishman. Be he alive or be he dead, I'll grind his bones to make my bread."

Enrichment Activities

- Reading details: have the children draw a picture of the three things that Jack took from the Giants' castle.
- Drawing conclusions: Why did Jack keep going back to the castle? The Giant fell to the earth. What do you think happened to his wife?

Script: Jack and the Beanstalk

SCENE 1: *(Outside Jack's cottage)*

CD TRACK 31: ..... *(MUSIC TO BEGIN THE STORY)*

Narrator: ...... Jack has a rope tied on their cow.

Jack: .... I don't want to sell her.

Jack's Mom: .. I don't want to sell her either. But, we need money to buy food.

Jack: .... What else could we sell?

Jack's Mom: .. We must sell the cow. She is all we have.

Jack: .... Ok. Come on Dolly, let's go. *(he leads the cow away)*

CD TRACK 32: ..... *(COW MOOING)*

Birds: .... Careful, Jack. Be careful!

SCENE 2: *(Jack's home)*

Narrator: ...... Jack arrives home, with a small bag. He looks very happy.

Jack: .... Mom! Mom! Guess what?

Jack's Mom: .. You got a good price for Dolly?

Jack: .... I got a great price for Dolly.

Jack's Mom: .. Well done, Jack! How much did you get?

Jack: .... We'll never be poor again!

Jack's Mom: .. Wow! Good old Dolly. Show me the money!

CD TRACK 33: ..... *(BEANS FALLING OUT)*

Narrator: ...... Jack empties the bag into his Mom's hand.

Jack's Mom: .. What do you call this!

Jack: .... They're Magic Beans! The man said we'll never be poor again.

Jack's Mom: ... You foolish boy! You were tricked! Now we have no cow and no money.

Narrator: ...... Jack's mother throws the beans out of the window. Then, she runs out in tears.

CD TRACK 34: ..... *(MOTHER CRYING)*

SCENE 3: *(Jack's home the next morning)*

Narrator: ...... The next morning Jack's Mom gets up. She sees the giant beanstalk in their yard.

Jack's Mom: .. Jack, wake up! Look at what you've done now!

Jack: .... What? What is it?

Jack's Mom: .. A horrid weed! It makes the whole house dark!

Jack: .... It's not a horrid weed! It's magic. Don't you see?

Jack's Mom: .. All is I see is a big ugly plant.

Jack: .... Let me see what's at the top.

Jack's Mom: .. You take care, Jack. It goes all the way to the sky.

Narrator: ...... Jack climbs until he's gone through the clouds. He is in another world! He sees a castle.

   CD TRACK 35: ..... *(LOUD KNOCKING, HUGE DOOR OPENS)*

Narrator: ...... Jack knocked on the door. A giant opens the huge door. He is so big he doesn't even see Jack.

Giant: .... Who is it? There's no one here. *(sniffs and smiles)* Fee Fi Fo Fum, I smell the blood of an Englishman. Be he alive or be he dead, I'll grind his bones to make my bread.

Jack: .... Yikes!

Narrator: ...... Jack runs through the Giant's legs and into the castle. He bumps into the Giant's Wife.

   CD TRACK 36: ..... *(FOOTSTEPS RUNNING, BUMPS INTO GIANT'S WIFE)*

Giant's Wife: *(bends down and looks at him)* Oh, how sweet! It's a tiny, tiny boy. I haven't seen one in years.

Giant: .... *(in another room)* Fee Fi Fo Fum, I smell the blood of an Englishman. Where is he?

Giant's Wife: . Hurry! He'll eat you! He loves to eat humans. Hide in my closet. Don't make a sound!

Narrator: ...... She pushes him into the closet.

   CD TRACK 37: ..... *(HUGE DOOR SHUTS)*

Birds: .... Careful, Jack. Be careful!

SCENE 4: *(Jack's home, his Mom is holding a golden coin)*

Jack's Mom:... If I didn't have this gold coin in my hand, I'd say you were lying. Castles in the sky? Giants? It's crazy.

Jack:............. Mom, I could go back for more. The closet was full of gold coins. The Giants won't know if a take a few more. The Giant's wife liked me.

Jack's Mom:... No, Jack. That would be greedy. With this coin, we can eat. We can even buy back Dolly. And, maybe buy some hens.

Jack:............. It was such fun! Nothing fun ever happens down here!

Jack's Mom:... I'm going to town with this coin. You stay here and wash the floor.

Jack:............. I've got time to go up before Mom gets back.

Narrator:...... Jack climbs up again. He knocks on the castle door.

CD TRACK 38:..... *(LOUD KNOCKING, HUGE DOOR OPENS)*

Narrator:...... The Giant opens the door and looks round. He doesn't see Jack. Once again, Jack runs through his legs.

Giant:........... Fee Fi Fo Fum, I smell the blood of an Englishman. Be he alive, or be he dead, I'll grind his bones to make my bread. Where is he?

Narrator:...... Jack runs into the hall, and again, bumps into the giant's wife.

CD TRACK 39:..... *(FOOTSTEPS RUNNING, BUMPS INTO GIANT'S WIFE)*

Giant's Wife:. There you are again, you cute little fella! You must stop coming here. My husband will eat you alive! Hurry, hide in my basket.

Jack:............. Can I go in the closet? I liked it in there.

Giant's Wife:. There's no time. He's coming! Quick!

Birds:............ Careful, Jack. Be careful!

SCENE 5: *(Jack's home)*

Narrator: ...... Jack is back at home with his mother. Now she is holding a golden egg.

Jack's Mom: .. If I didn't have this egg in my hand, I'd say you were lying. Hens that lay golden eggs? Crazy.

Jack: .... The Giant's wife hid me in her basket. She put the basket in the yard. I saw the hen lay a golden egg. So, when she went out, I picked up the hen and ran.

Jack's Mom: .. Jack, we will never be poor again. So, never go back up that beanstalk.

CD TRACK 40: ..... *(HEN CLUCKING)*

Birds: .... Careful, Jack. Be careful!

SCENE 6: *(Jack's home)*

Narrator: ...... Jack is home alone —and bored.

Jack: .... Just one more time!

Narrator: ...... Jack climbs up the beanstalk and goes to the castle.

CD TRACK 41: ..... *(LOUD KNOCKING, HUGE DOOR OPENS)*

Narrator: ...... He knocks at the door. The Giant opens the door and does not see Jack.

Giant: .... *(Giant sniffs)* Fee Fi Fo Fum, I smell the blood of an Englishman. Be he alive, or be he dead, I'll grind his bones to make my bread.

Narrator: ...... Jack runs through the door and bumps into the Giant's wife.

CD TRACK 42: ..... *(FOOTSTEPS RUNNING, BUMPS INTO GIANT'S WIFE)*

Giant's Wife: . You again! You are so cute! I might eat you. Quick – the Giant's coming. Hide under the table.

CD TRACK 43: ..... *(GIANT'S HUGE FOOTSTEPS)*

Giant: .... Wife. There's a human! I know there's a human. You're not hiding one are you?

Giant's Wife: . No, my dear. Now calm down.

Giant:............How can I calm down? I know there's a human, but I can't find him. This is what drives hungry giants crazy.

Giant's Wife:.. Sit down. Let your magic harp play music for you. That will help calm you down.

Giant:............Very well.

Narrator:...... The Giant sits down. The harp in the corner of the room starts to play music all on its own.

CD TRACK 44:..... *(HARP MUSIC)*

Giant:............But I'm in a bad, bad mood wife.

Birds:..............Careful, Jack. Be careful!

SCENE 7: *(Jack's home)*

Narrator:...... Jack is back home with his mom. She's holding the golden harp. The beanstalk has been cut down and the Giant is lying on the ground, dead.

Jack's Mom:.. If this Giant wasn't dead at my feet, and this harp wasn't in my hand, I'd say you were lying.

Jack:..............You should have seen me run! When the Giant and his wife fell asleep, I grabbed the harp and ran!

Jack's Mom:.. But he woke up and chased you down the beanstalk?

Jack:..............Yes! I didn't think he could run that fast.

Jack's Mom:.. So, you cut down the beanstalk. Then, the Giant fell all the way down.

Jack:..............Yep. Are you proud of me?

Jack's Mom:.. Well, you have been brave, and we'll never be poor again, but. . .

Jack:..............But, what?

Jack's Mom:.. You were greedy. You kept going back when we didn't need it.

Jack:..............But, it was fun! I'm bored here.

Jack's Mom:.. I know Jack, that's why I've found you a job.

Jack:..............What? A job? Where?

Jack's Mom:.. The man who sold you the magic beans told me about it. He's a nice man. In fact, he's taking me to dinner tonight.

Jack:.............. Told you about what? Where will I work?

Jack's Mom:.. You are going to work in a nursing home. A nursing home for sick, old giants.

Jack:.............. You must be kidding!

Jack's Mom:.. Don't worry – none of them have any teeth. They are also sorry about eating humans. You'll have a lovely time.

Birds:............. Careful, Jack. Be careful!

THE END

Jack and the Beanstalk Prop Patterns

Directions: Copy, color, cut out, and laminate for durability.

Magic beans

Coins

Jack and the Beanstalk Prop Patterns

Directions: Copy, color, cut out, and laminate for durability.

Golden egg

Hen

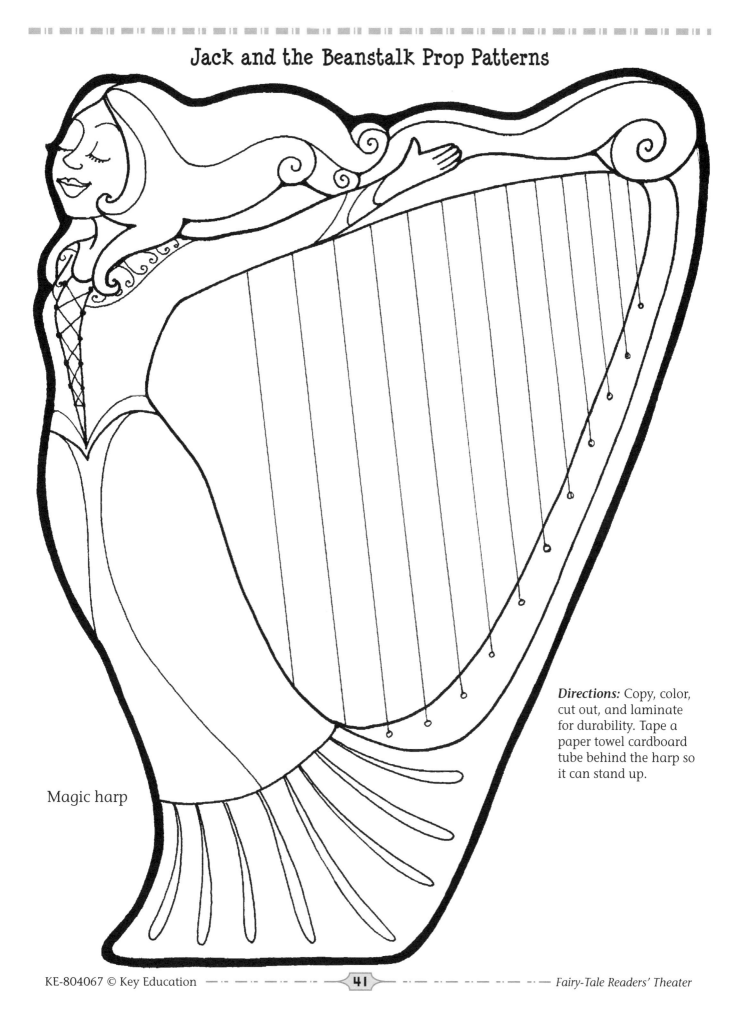

Directions: Copy, color, cut out, and laminate for durability. Tape a paper towel cardboard tube behind the harp so it can stand up.

Magic harp

Hansel and Gretel

PERFORMANCE PREPARATION SCRIPT AND PROPS

Characters and Reading Levels

Hansel and Gretel includes six characters and a group choral reading.

- Hansel ....reading level 2.1
- Gretel ....reading level 2.5
- Father ....reading level 2.0
- Stepmother ....reading level 1.9
- Witch ....reading level 2.3
- Narrator ....reading level 2.5
- Forest Trees (group).... reading level 1.8

The "Forest Trees" choral reading can be read by a small or a large group—allowing the entire class to participate. You may also choose to eliminate the choral reading. Make a single copy of the script and "white-out" the lines of the "Forest Trees." Then, copy the edited script for the six performing story characters.

Reproducible Script and Props

- Reproduce the script: *Hansel and Gretel,* found on pages 43–47 for each student.
- Make the story props—patterns and directions are found on pages 48–50.

Audio CD Sound Effects

- Sound effects for *Hansel and Gretel,* are found on tracks 45–55. Directions for when to play each sound effect can be found in the script.

Optional Costume & Set Suggestions

- Witch's candy house: Use a large cardboard box, paint white, and then paint on candy and glue on candy wrappers.
- Forest trees: Make large cardboard stand up trees or paint a mural of a forest scene to use as a background.
- An extra fun touch is to make bird cut outs. Attach strings so they can fly down to eat the bread crumbs.
- Characters: black witch dress and regular clothing for the rest of the cast.

READING PREPARATION AND ENRICHMENT ACTIVITIES

Review the Traditional Story

- *Hansel and Gretel* by Rika Lesser and Paul O. Zelinsky. Dutton Juvenile (1999)
- *Hansel and Gretel* by James Marshall. Puffin (1994)
- *Hansel & Gretel* by Will Moses. Philomel (2006)
- *Hansel and Gretel: A Retelling of the Grimms' Fairy Tale* (Read-It! Readers) by Eric Blair, Wilhelm Grimm, Jacob Grimm, and Claudia Wolf. Picture Window Books (2004)

Teach New Vocabulary

Teach the following vocabulary (word recognition and meaning) prior to reading the script: *bright, children, crumbs, fatten, follow, Gretel, Hansel, peace, quiet, stepmother, stones, trail, whispering, witch, wolves.*

Encourage Fluency

- First, read through the script without using any of the props.
- The teacher makes a tape recording for the children to use for practice. The children can track the text and read-along with the teacher's voice.
- Over-pronouncing is a good exercise to use to improve fluency. The Forest trees group reading is the same line throughout the script and can be very effective when it is over-pronounced. Have all the students practice this technique using the line, "We wouldn't be so sure about that!"

Enrichment Activities

- Inference: There is a surprise ending *(the witch is the stepmother's mom).* Discuss this ending. Could this be why the stepmother was so mean?"
- Have the children dictate this story. Write it on chart paper using the children's own words. Read it together as a class. Add illustrations and turn into a classroom big book.

Script: Hansel and Gretel

SCENE 1: *(In a poor cottage)*

CD TRACK 45: ..... *(MUSIC TO BEGIN THE STORY)*

Narrator: ...... Hansel and Gretel work hard doing their jobs. The Stepmother and Father are whispering in a corner.

Stepmother: .. If I feed them, there's none left for me! They've got to go.

Father: .... Got to go?! They are my children!

Stepmother: .. Well, they are not mine. And, they eat too much food.

Father: .... I will ask them not to eat so much. Please, let them stay.

Stepmother: .. No! My mind is made up. You must take them deep into the woods. Then, light a fire and leave them there.

Hansel: .... *(whispers to Gretel)* Did you hear them? She wants to get rid of us.

Gretel: .... Dad won't let her.

Hansel: .... You think? He does what she tells him.

Gretel: .... Don't worry, Hansel. Dad would never leave us in the woods.

CD TRACK 46: ..... *(FOREST SOUNDS)*

Forest Trees: .. We wouldn't be so sure about that!

SCENE 2: *(Later, in the cottage)*

Father: .... Hey kids, how about a walk in the forest?

Hansel/Gretel: ...No, thanks!

Stepmother: ....A walk in the woods would be nice. Your father can make you a fire.

Hansel/Gretel: ...No, thanks!

Father: .... Maybe the kids are right. We won't go.

Stepmother: .. Oh, yes you will! I need some peace and quiet. Now go!

Hansel/Gretel: ...*(whispering)* Dad will not leave us!

CD TRACK 47: ..... *(FOREST SOUNDS)*

Forest Trees: .. We wouldn't be so sure about that!

SCENE 3: *(In the forest, at night)*

Gretel: .... What do we do now? No food and no way home. We'll be eaten by bears.

Hansel: .... No, we won't.

Gretel: .... Or wolves.

Hansel: .... No, we won't.

Gretel: .... Or pigs.

Hansel: .... Pigs?! No, we won't.

Gretel: .... How can you be sure?

Hansel: .... We can find our way back home. I made a trail with white stones from home to here.

Narrator: ...... The children start to follow the white stone trail back home.

Gretel: .... Did I ever tell you how great you are?

Hansel: .... No.

Gretel: .... Well, you are.

Hansel: .... Thanks.

Gretel: .... Hansel? Have you got any food?

Hansel: .... No.

Gretel: .... Well, you're not that great then.

SCENE 4: *(The next night)*

Narrator: ..... Hansel and Gretel made it back home. Now, their father wants to take them back into the woods.

Gretel: .... Dad, why are you taking us into the woods again?

Father: .... Your Stepmother needs a bit of peace. Please, don't make this hard for me.

Hansel: .... Hard for you? What about us? We're the ones being left in the woods!

Father: .... You'll be fine.

CD TRACK 48: ..... *(FOREST SOUNDS)*

Forest Trees: .. We wouldn't be so sure about that!

Narrator: ...... Again, the Father leaves Hansel and Gretel in the woods.

Gretel: .... Did you bring the stones again?

Hansel: .... No, she was watching me. But, I saved my bread and used that.

Gretel: .... Did I ever tell you how great you are?

Hansel: .... Just once, I think.

Gretel: .... Well, you are! Come on, let's go home. I'm hungry.

Narrator: ...... The children start looking for the bread crumbs.

    CD TRACK 49: ..... *(MANY BIRDS CHIRPING)*

Hansel: .... On no! The birds must have eaten the bread. It's all gone.

Gretel: .... Maybe you're not that great. What do we do now?

Hansel: .... Let's walk and hope we find home.

    CD TRACK 50: ..... *(FOREST SOUNDS)*

Forest Trees: .. We wouldn't be so sure about that!

SCENE 5: *(Night in the forest)*

Narrator: ...... The children walk all night. It starts to get light. They come to a bright house.

Gretel: .... Wow! Look at this house?

Hansel: .... It's made of candy!

Gretel: .... Amazing!

Narrator: ...... The children begin to eat parts of the house.

    CD TRACK 51: ..... *(DOOR OPENS, THEN CLOSES)*

Narrator: ...... Suddenly, there stands an old, old woman.

Witch: .... *(in a kind voice)* Come in children. You must be hungry. Come in and eat.

Gretel: .... Thank you. We LOVE your house.

Hansel: .... And, we are very hungry.

Narrator: ...... The children go in the house. The door shuts and the witch pushes Hansel into a cage.

CD TRACK 52: ..... *(DOOR SLAMS SHUT, BOY SCREAMS)*

Witch: .... You are not as hungry as I am! I haven't eaten a child in weeks. Boy, you're a bit thin! I'll have to fatten you up.

Gretel: .... How dare you! Let him out now!

Witch: .... Sorry little lady, but I'm the one who is the boss. Now, make me some tea. Give the boy some food, too!

SCENE 6: *(Three weeks later)*

Narrator: ...... It is three weeks later. Hansel is in the cage. Gretel is whispering to him through the bars. The witch is asleep in a chair.

CD TRACK 53: ..... *(SNORING)*

Hansel: .... We have got to get out of here. The witch has been trying to fatten me up for weeks.

Gretel: .... She still thinks you are too thin. She can't see very well. You hold out that bone and she thinks it's your finger.

Hansel: .... SShhh! She's waking up!

Witch: .... I'm sick of this! Fat or thin, I'm going to eat you boy!

CD TRACK 54: ..... *(FOREST SOUNDS)*

Forest Trees: .. We wouldn't be so sure about that!

Witch: .... Girl—check if the oven is hot.

Gretel: .... I can't tell if it's hot. Can you show me? *(Gretel winks at Hansel)*

Witch: .... Stupid girl. It's easy. You just lean inside…

Narrator: .... Gretel pushes the witch in the oven. Then, she slams the door shut.

Hansel: .... Yes! You did it!

Gretel: .... Now, the key . . . oh no . . .

Hansel: .... What?

Gretel: .... The key was in her pocket!

Hansel: .... Look! What's that on the floor?

Gretel: .... It's the key! It must have fallen out when I pushed her in the oven.

Narrator:	Gretel lets Hansel out of the cage.
Hansel:	Before we go, let's break down the house. We can take the candy home.
Gretel:	Have I ever told you how great you are?
Hansel:	A couple of times.

<u>SCENE 7:</u> *(Walking home in the forest)*

Narrator:	The children walk home. It takes a long time, but they finally get there.
Hansel:	Don't forget Gretel, no more walks in the woods with Dad.
Gretel:	Deal.
Narrator:	The children are home. They run into the house and hug their father.
Father:	My dear children! You're back!
Gretel:	Yes, we are! We are not going for any more walks in the woods.
Hansel:	Not ever.
Father:	Don't worry. Your Stepmother is not here.
Gretel:	Where is she?
Father:	She had some bad news. Her mother died.
Hansel:	I didn't know she had a mother.
Father:	Her mother lived on the other side of the woods. You won't believe this—she fell into her own oven!
Gretel:	Really?
Father:	And someone knocked down her house.
Hansel:	Really?
Gretel:	How awful!
Father:	Yes, but there is some good news. I have told your Stepmother never to come back. You mean more to me than her.
CD TRACK 55:	*(FOREST SOUNDS)*
Forest Trees: ..	We are sure about that!
Gretel/Hansel: ...	Thanks, Dad. Want some candy?

THE END

Hansel and Gretel Prop Patterns

White stones

Directions: Copy, color, cut out, and laminate for durability.

Key to Hansel's cage

Bread

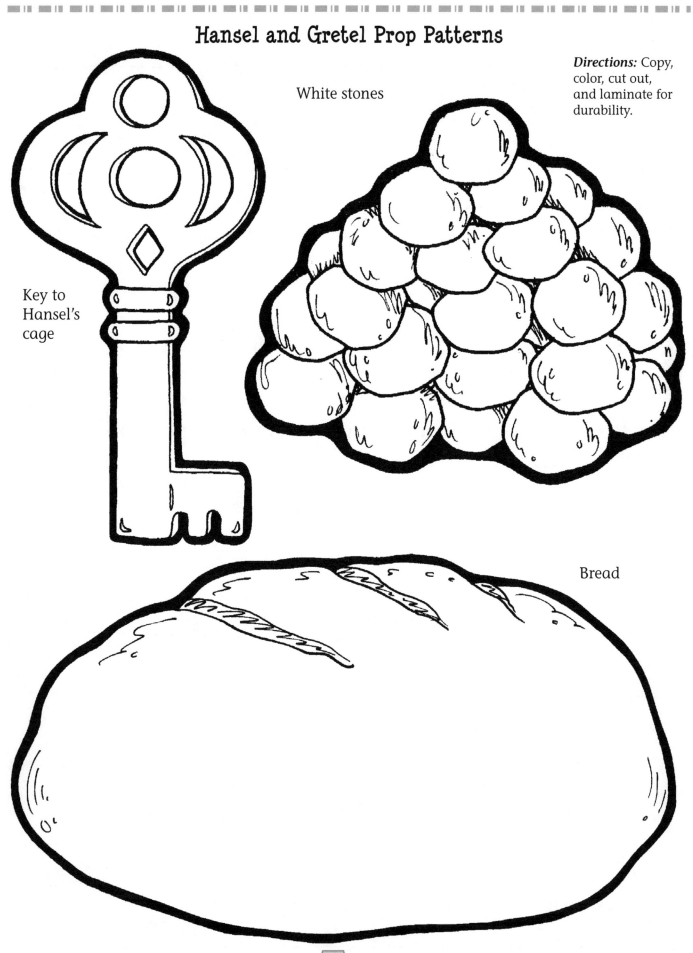

Hansel and Gretel Prop Patterns

Directions: Copy, color, cut out, and laminate for durability.

Bone that Hansel holds out to the witch

Candy brought home by Hansel and Gretel

Hansel and Gretel
Prop Patterns

Witch mask

(cut out)   (cut out)

Directions: Copy, color, cut out, and laminate for durability. Cut out eye holes. Tape a construction paper strip from the left side to the right side of the mask so that it fits the child's head comfortably.

The Pied Piper of Hamelin

PERFORMANCE PREPARATION SCRIPT AND PROPS

Characters and Reading Levels

The Pied Piper of Hamelin includes seven characters and a group choral reading.

- Mayor......................... reading level 2.4
- Piper .... reading level 2.5
- Fred............................ reading level 2.1
- Doris........................... reading level 2.2
- Jon .... reading level 2.2
- Susan......................... reading level 2.0
- Narrator .... reading level 2.7
- Crowd (group)............ reading level 1.9

The "Crowd" choral reading can be read by a small or a large group—allowing the entire class to participate. You may also choose to eliminate the choral reading. Make a single copy of the script and "white-out" the lines of the "Crowd." Then, copy the edited script for the seven performing story characters.

Reproducible Script and Props

- Reproduce the script: *The Pied Piper of Hamelin*, found on pages 52–57 for each student.
- Make the story props—patterns and directions are found on pages 56–65.

Audio CD Sound Effects

- Sound effects for *The Pied Piper of Hamelin*, are found on tracks 60–70. Directions for when to play each sound effect can be found in the script.

Optional Costume & Set Suggestions

- Rats: Create a "rat train" that the piper can pull off the stage. Make several copies of the rats on pages 58 and 59. Color, cut out, and glue each rat to a side of a small box. connect all the boxes with strings. The Piper can hold the first string and pull the rats out of town.
- Characters: everyday clothing except for a suit for the Major, bright and odd clothing for the Piper.

READING PREPARATION AND ENRICHMENT ACTIVITIES

Review the Traditional Story

- *The Pied Piper of Hamelin* by Robert Browning. Everyman's Library (1993)
- *The Pied Piper of Hamelin* by Robert Holden and Drahos Zak. Houghton Mifflin (1998)
- *Pied Piper of Hamelin* by Ladybird Books. (1998)
- *The Pied Piper of Peru* by Ann Tompert and Kestutis Kasparavicius. Boyds Mills Press (2002)
- *The Boy Who Was Followed Home* by Margaret Mahy and Steven Kellogg. Puffin (1993)

Teach New Vocabulary

Teach the following vocabulary (word recognition and meaning) prior to reading the script: *baby-sitter, crowd, ducats (term used for Hamelin's currency), flute, Hamelin, hooray, hundred, Mayor, morning, nasty, pied, pipe, Piper, quitter, townspeople.*

Encourage Fluency

- First, read through the script without using any of the props.
- Chunking is when a group of words are spoken in rhythm in a phrase. The crowd lines are perfect for practicing this skill becasue of the repetition, for example, "Major, get rid of the rats! Get rid of the rats! Get rid of the rats!"
- There are also many exclaimation marks in this script. The people are excited, scared, and worried. Point this out to the children. Practice reading some of the lines with exclaimation marks to show the children how they need to voice excitement, anger, etc.

Enrichment Activities

- Drawing conclusions: Why did all the rats come to Hamelin? What do you think happened to the Mayor? The Piper? Did the Piper ever come back to baby-sit? Was the Piper's flute magic?

Script: The Pied Piper of Hamelin

SCENE 1: (*In the Town Hall of Hamelin*)

CD TRACK 56: ..... (*MUSIC TO BEGIN THE STORY*)

Narrator: . The Town Hall of Hamelin was full of people. The people were very unhappy.

CD TRACK 57: ..... (*ANGRY CROWD SOUNDS*)

Mayor: ..... We have to get rid of these rats!

Fred: .... Tell us something we don't know!

Doris: .... That is all we have done for the past six weeks.

Jon: .... We've put down rat traps!

Susan: ...... And poison!

Fred: .... We've put food for them outside the town!

Doris: .... My mom even sang to them!

Jon: .... She sounds like a dying dog. Even that trick didn't work.

Mayor: ..... Then, we must try something new.

Susan: ...... Yes, we know that! We just don't know what to do. You are the Mayor! You tell us what to try next.

Fred: .... You are not much of a Mayor if you can't fix this.

Mayor: ..... How dare you talk to me like that! I'm the Mayor of Hamelin.

Doris: .... You need to get rid of the rats!

Jon: .... If the rats don't go, maybe you will.

Susan: ...... Yes, what do you all think?

Crowd: ..... Mayor, get rid of the rats! Get rid of the rats! Get rid of the rats!

CD TRACK 58: ..... (*ANGRY CROWD SOUNDS*)

SCENE 2: *(Mayor's Office)*

Narrator: . The Mayor is in his office. His head is in his hands. Every so often he knocks a rat off his desk. Then, there is a knock at the door.

CD TRACK 59: ..... *(KNOCKING ON DOOR)*

Mayor: ..... Come in.

Narrator: . A man in very bright clothes walks in. He is holding a flute.

Piper: .... Good morning, Mayor. It is a fine day.

Mayor: ..... Don't stand there and waste my time. What do you want?

Piper: .... To help you.

Mayor: ..... You can help me by going away. I have a lot on my mind. I need time to think.

Piper: .... You need to get rid of the rats. I can do that.

Mayor: ..... How do you know about the rats?

Narrator: . A rat runs across the Mayor's desk.

Piper: .... Everyone knows about the rats.

Mayor: ..... Really? You say you can get rid of them?

Piper: .... Yep. Easy Peasy, Lemon Squeezy.

Mayor: ..... How?

Piper: .... *(he holds up the pipe)* With this little baby.

CD TRACK 60: ..... *(FLUTE MUSIC)*

Mayor: ..... Stop talking like a fool. I'm the Mayor! Show me some respect.

Piper: .... If you are going to be nasty, I'll go. You can get rid of your own rats.

Mayor: ..... No! Don't go! Tell me how you plan to get rid of them.

Piper: .... You will have to pay me.

Mayor: ..... If you can get rid of the rats, I'll pay you a hundred ducats.

Piper: .... I know I can get rid of them.

Mayor: ..... Then, it's a deal. *(They shake hands)*

Piper: .... Ok – let's get this party started . . .

Crowd: ..... Piper, get rid of the rats! Get rid of the rats! Get rid of the rats!

SCENE 3: *(In the Town Hall the next day)*

Crowd: ..... What is the Piper going to do?!

Fred: .... What? He will play his pipe and the rats will follow him out of town!

Mayor: ..... Trust me. He is a good man.

Doris: .... Well, I say let him try.

Jon: .... I found a rat in my bed last night!

Susan: ...... I'm sick of it, too. There was a rat in my toilet today!

Mayor: ..... Then, it's final. I will tell the Piper to do it in the morning.

Doris: .... Will you pay him?

Mayor: ..... Yes, it's all taken care of.

Crowd: ..... Hooray for the Major! Hooray for the Major! Hooray for the Major!

    CD TRACK 61: ..... *(CROWD CHEERING)*

SCENE 4: *(In the Mayor's office the next afternoon)*

Narrator: . The next day the Piper went to see the Major. He came to get his money.

Piper: .... You said you would pay me a hundred ducats.

Mayor: ..... I don't think I did.

Piper: .... But you did. I said I'd get rid of the rats, and I did. You said you'd pay me—so pay me!

Mayor: ..... My dear man, calm down. Tooting into that silly pipe is not worth a hundred ducats. I'll give you ten.

Piper: .... Ten?! I got rid of all the rats. They jumped into the lake. They are gone. Now, pay me the money, Honey.

Mayor: ..... I have two things to say to you. One, don't ever call me Honey. And two, get out!

Piper: .... You will wish you hadn't said that.

    CD TRACK 62: ..... *(DOOR SLAMS SHUT)*

SCENE 5: *(Hamelin town square)*

Narrator: . The townspeople are outside talking. They are talking about the Piper.

CD TRACK 63: ..... *(CROWD TALKING)*

Fred: .... I have never seen anything like it! He played his pipe and the rats followed him out of town.

Doris: .... Then, the rats jumped into the lake! Just like they were going for a swim.

Jon: .... He was great! I wish we could thank him The Mayor said he had to rush off.

Susan: ...... That's too bad.

Narrator: . The Mayor runs into the room. He is in a panic.

Mayor: ..... Help! Help!

Fred: .... What's up?

Mayor: ..... That evil man! How could he do this to Hamelin?

Doris: .... Slow down. What did he do?

Mayor: ..... He has taken the children. With his pipe! He has led all the children away! We don't know where they are!

Jon: .... Do we know where the Piper is?

Mayor: ..... No.

Susan: ...... Why would he so such a thing?

Mayor: ..... I have no idea. He is just a bad man. *(coughs)*

Crowd: ..... Where are the children? Where are the children? Where are the children?

CD TRACK 64: ..... *(ANGRY CROWD SOUNDS)*

SCENE 6: *(Looking for the children)*

Narrator: . The townspeople and the Mayor need help to find the children. The Piper comes back to town. The Mayor sees the Piper and tries to leave.

Mayor: ..... I think I will go. I will look somewhere else for the children.

Fred: .... Don't go! You need to talk to the Piper.

Doris: .... He has to tell us where the children are.

Mayor: ..... You go ask him. I want to go look for the children.

Narrator: . The Piper walks up to the townspeople.

Jon: .... What have you done with our children?

Susan: ...... You are a nasty man.

Piper: .... Me, nasty?! You are the nasty ones!

Fred: .... What are you talking about? You have taken our children away.

Piper: .... You said you would pay me—and you didn't!

Doris: .... Didn't pay you? Of course, we did—didn't we, Mayor?

Mayor: ..... errrr... I did pay him. He just wanted more.

Piper: .... The Mayor said he'd pay me a HUNDRED ducats. He only gave me TEN.

Jon: .... Mayor, why did you do that?

Mayor: ..... It looked so easy. It seemed like too much pay.

Susan: ...... You are a mean old man! Give the Piper his money.

Fred: .... And then, can we get the children back?

Piper: .... Yes, that's right. They are very safe.

Crowd: ..... Pay the Piper! Pay the Piper! Pay the Piper!

CD TRACK 65: ..... *(ANGRY CROWD SOUNDS)*

SCENE 7: *(At the edge of the town)*

Narrator: . The Piper, Fred, Doris, Susan, and Jon are on the edge of the town.

Piper: .... I am glad this has a happy ending.

Doris: .... It has worked out well for all of us. The rats are gone!

Jon:........... The Mayor is gone! And soon, the children will be back.

Piper: .... I'll go and get them now. You will hear us coming over the hill.

Susan: ...... So, the children have been happy?

Piper: .... Oh, very happy.

Fred:......... And safe?

Piper: .... Very safe. We have had a lot of fun.

Doris: .... Maybe you can come back and take the children again! Just for a few days.

Crowd: ..... Glad the Piper was no quitter. Now, he is our baby-sitter!

THE END

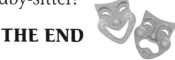

The Pied Piper of Hamelin Prop Patterns

Directions: Copy, color, cut out, and laminate for durability. The child reading the role of the Mayor can place double stick tape on the back of the mustache to hold it in place.

Mayor's Mustache

The Pied Piper of Hamelin Prop Patterns

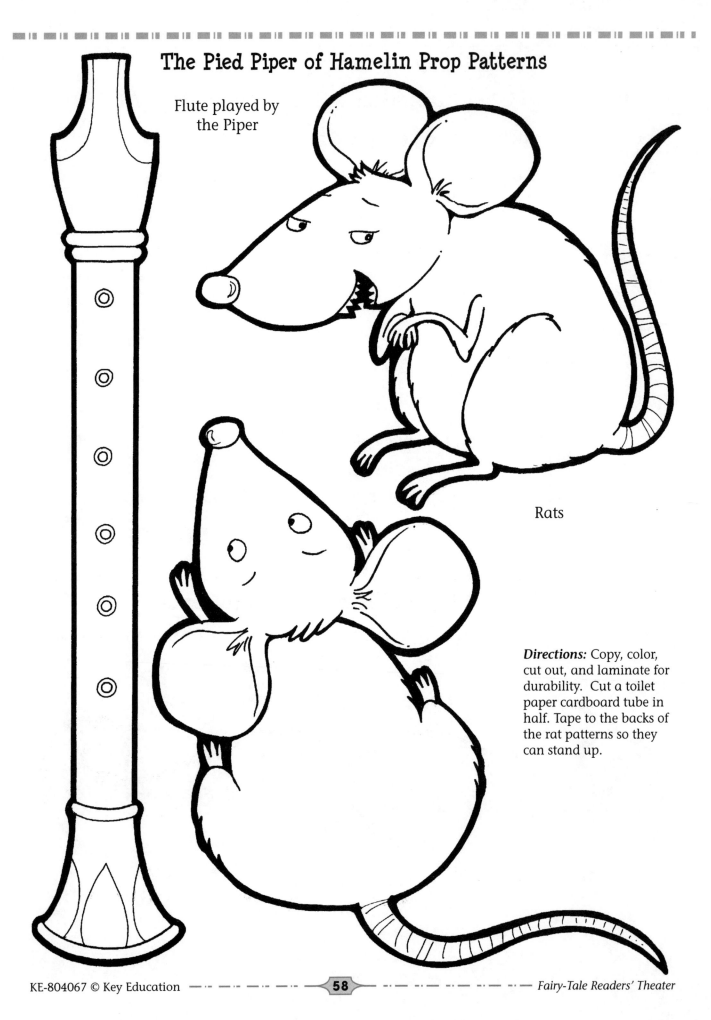

Flute played by
the Piper

Rats

Directions: Copy, color,
cut out, and laminate for
durability. Cut a toilet
paper cardboard tube in
half. Tape to the backs of
the rat patterns so they
can stand up.

Rats

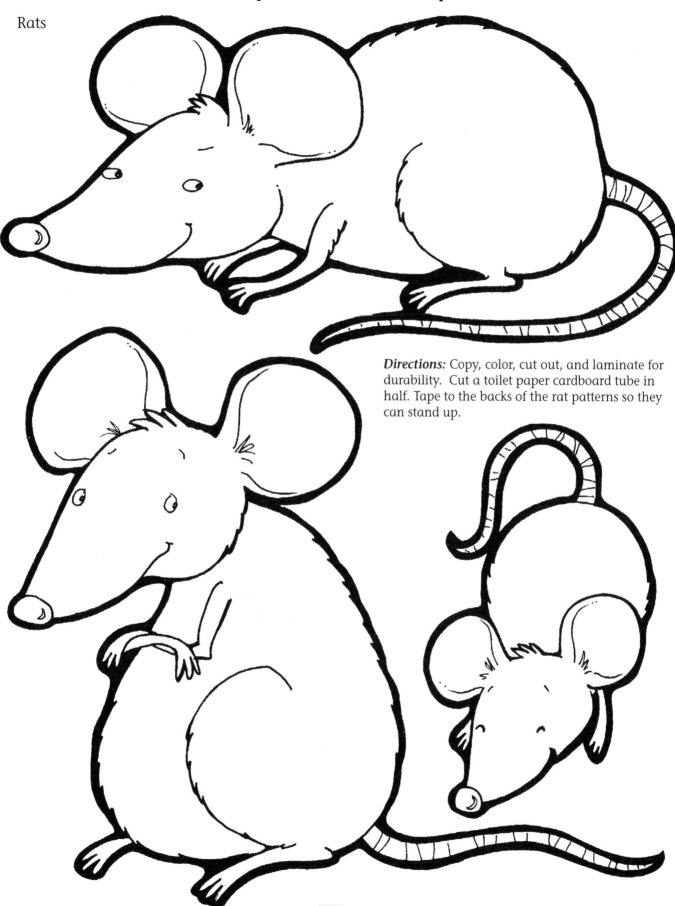

Directions: Copy, color, cut out, and laminate for durability. Cut a toilet paper cardboard tube in half. Tape to the backs of the rat patterns so they can stand up.

Little Red Riding Hood

PERFORMANCE PREPARATION SCRIPT AND PROPS

Characters and Reading Levels

Little Red Riding Hood includes five characters and a group choral reading.

- Red Riding Hood .... reading level 2.1
- Red Riding Hood's Mom reading level 1.8
- Wolf .... reading level 2.5
- Gran .... reading level 2.2
- Narrator .... reading level 2.7
- Forest Animals (group) reading level 2.0

The "Forest Animals" choral reading can be read by a small or a large group—allowing the entire class to participate. You may also choose to eliminate the choral reading. Make a single copy of the script and "white-out" the lines of the "Forest Animals." Then, copy the edited script for the six performing story characters.

Reproducible Script and Props

- Reproduce the script: *Little Red Riding Hood,* found on pages 61–66 for each student.
- Make the story props—patterns and directions are found on pages 66–68.

Audio CD Sound Effects

- Sound effects for *Little Red Riding Hood,* are found on tracks 66–73. Directions for when to play each sound effect can be found in the script.

Optional Costume & Set Suggestions

- Wolf: gray or black pants and shirt; copy the wolf mask on gray card stock, glue on fur or small pieces of gray and black yarn; nightgown and bed cap for later in the story
- Red Riding Hood: red cape, dress, basket filled with food
- Gran: nightgown, bed cap
- Other props: table and chairs, small table to be used as Gran's bed; forest mural or cardboard stand up trees

READING PREPARATION AND ENRICHMENT ACTIVITIES

Review the Traditional Story

- *Little Red Riding Hood* by Candice Ransom. Brighter Child (2001)
- *Little Red Riding Hood* by Jerry Pinkney. Little, Brown Young Readers (2007)
- *Red Riding Hood* by Charles Perrault and James Marshall. Picture Puffins (1993)
- *Little Red Riding Hood* by Jacob Grimm, Wilhelm Grimm, and Trina Schart Hyman. Holiday House (1987)
- *Little Red Riding Hood: A Newfangled Prairie Tale* (Stories to Go!) by Lisa Campbell. Aladdin (2005)

Teach New Vocabulary

Teach the following vocabulary (word recognition and meaning) prior to reading the script: *admit, better, brothers, careful, edge, flesh, Gran, Granny, lovely, meaty, mighty, nothing, polite, Red Riding Hood, scare, sisters, sneaking, stronger, tasty, wolf*

Encourage Fluency

- First, read through the script without using any of the props.
- Peer-reading is an excellent tool for helping children improve fluency. Use Scene 4 (page 63) for children to practice reading with a partner. It is the famous scene when Red Riding Hood discovers the wolf in her Grandma's bed.
- The Forest Animals' group readings are warnings. They should be spoken with worry and concern. Most of these lines also rhyme thereby adding a rhythm, which can help children read smoothly.

Enrichment Activities

- Compare and contrast: In this version, Red Riding Hood wants to be tough and strong and the Wolf is trying to help Red Riding Hood's mother. Using Venn diagrams—compare and contrast this version of Red Riding Hood and the Wolf with other more traditional versions of these characters.

Script: Little Red Riding Hood

SCENE 1: *(Red Riding Hood's house)*

CD TRACK 66: ..... *(MUSIC TO BEGIN THE STORY)*

Narrator: ....Little Red Riding Hood is at home with her mother. She is getting ready to take food to her sick Gran.

Mother: ....Is the bag too heavy?

Red Riding: ....No, mom.

Mother: ....It's a long walk to Gran's house.

Red Riding: ....Mom, don't fuss. I'm strong.

Mother: ....You are my little girl. I worry about you.

Red Riding: ....Look, Mom! I'm taller than you! I can pick you up.

Narrator: ....Little Red Riding Hood picks up her mother.

Mother: ....Put me down! Right now!

Red Riding: ....See Mom, I am strong. I am stronger than any boy in my class.

Mother: ....That's no way for a pretty girl to talk! Now, put on your red coat and get going. Your Gran needs that food. She is not well.

Red Riding: ....Ok. I will be back before dark. Bye.

CD TRACK 67: ..... *(DOOR OPENS, THEN CLOSES)*

Forest Animals: ...Be careful, Little Red Riding Hood. The Wolf is in the woods!

SCENE 2: *(Red Riding Hood walking in the woods)*

CD TRACK 68: ..... *(FOREST SOUNDS)*

Narrator: ....Little Red Riding Hood is walking in the woods. The Wolf has been watching her. Now, he comes up and talks to her.

Wolf: ....Hello, little girl. How are you today?

Red Riding: ....I'm fine, but I'm not little. You sound like my Mom!

Wolf: ....Where are you going with all that food?

Red Riding:.........To see my Gran. She is sick.

Wolf:....................What's wrong with her?

Red Riding:.........She can't see very well. She can't hear very well. And, now she has a bad cold.

Wolf:....................You must be tired, little girl. Let me help you. That basket looks heavy.

Red Riding:.........No, thanks. I'm not tired at all.

Wolf:....................Oh yes, look at your lovely, meaty arms. A lot of nice flesh on them. Mmmm.

Red Riding:.........I have to go. Gran lives at the edge of the woods. I need to go now.

Wolf:....................Does she live in that little house by the lake?

Red Riding:.........Yes, that's the one.

Wolf:....................Well, you had better go.

Narrator: ....The Wolf runs off to Gran's house. But, he goes a different way.

Red Riding:.........*(Speaking to herself in Wolf's voice)* "You must be tired, little girl." One day, I'll show them. I'm not little and I'm not weak!

Forest Animals:..Be careful, Little Red Riding Hood. The Wolf is in the woods!

SCENE 3: *(Gran's house)*

Narrator: ....The Wolf is at Gran's house. She hears a knock at the door.

   CD TRACK 69:.....*(KNOCKING ON DOOR)*

Gran:....................Hello? Who's there?

Wolf:....................*(in high voice)* Granny, it's me! I have some food for you.

Gran:....................*(to herself)* Why is she talking in that silly voice? She never calls me Granny. *(calls out)* Who is it? I can't hear very well.

Forest Animals:..Gran, you should shout. The Wolf is sneaking about!

Wolf:....................It's me, Granny darling, Little Red Riding Hood. Can I come in?

Gran: .... You know the door is open. Come in.

Wolf: .... *(Wolf talk in his own voice)* Hello, Granny. Oops!

Gran: .... Oops? What do you mean? Who are you?

Wolf: .... I was hoping to eat you first. Then, I will eat that tasty little girl. But, you are too skinny.

Gran: .... How rude. You won't be able to eat Little Red Riding Hood. She is very strong. And, she won't be bossed around by you!

Wolf: .... First, I will lock you in a closet. Then, I will have to trick her.

Narrator: .... He picks up Gran and puts her in the closet.

Gran: .... Get your paws off me! You won't get away with this. You look nothing like me!

Forest Animals: .. Poor Gran is locked away! Can Little Red Riding Hood save the day?

SCENE 4: *(Red Riding Hood arrives at Gran's house)*

Narrator: .... Little Red Riding Hood knocks on the door. The Wolf is in bed wearing one of Gran's hats. Little Red Riding Hood lets herself in.

CD TRACK 70: .... *(KNOCKING ON DOOR)*

Red Riding: .... Hi, Gran. I have some food for you.

Wolf: .... Thank you! I am very hungry.

Red Riding: .... Gran – you look weird. Are you ok?

Wolf: .... I will be when I get a nice big hug from you. Come here.

Forest Animals: .. Little Red Riding Hood open your eyes. You are in for a big surprise!

CD TRACK 71: ..... *(EVIL MUSIC)*

Red Riding: .... *(goes to the bed)* Hang on! You're not Gran. You have such big ears!

Wolf: .... All the better to hear you with.

Red Riding: .... And such big eyes!

Wolf:....................All the better to see you with.

Red Riding:.........And such big teeth! You're not Gran! You're that wolf! And, you want to eat me with your big teeth!

Wolf:....................Hey! I was suppose to say that.

Red Riding:.........There's no way you're going to eat me. Or my Gran. Where is she?

Wolf:....................Don't worry. I'm not going to eat her. She's too thin. I locked her in the closet.

Red Riding:.........I'm coming Gran!

Narrator: ....Little Red Riding Hood runs over to the closet to let Gran out. The Wolf leaps out of bed to stop her. But, he trips over the dress he is wearing.

   CD TRACK 72:..... *(CRASHING SOUND)*

Wolf:....................Ouch! Stupid dress.

Gran:...................*(Coming out of the closet)* That's my girl!

Red Riding:.........Are you ok?

Gran:...................I'm fine now that you are here. I knew you were stronger than that silly Wolf.

Wolf:....................You only got out of the closet because I tripped over my nightie.

Gran:................... That's MY nightie.

Wolf:....................Your nightie?

Red Riding:.........So, do you want to see how strong I am?

Wolf:....................No. I just want to eat you.

Red Riding:.........Just try it—you big ball of fur!

Gran:...................Yea, just try it—you hairy goof ball.

Wolf:....................Right. You asked for it.

Narrator: ....The Wolf grabs Little Red Riding Hood's arm, but she grabs his paws. The Wolf tries to get free but her grip is too strong.

   CD TRACK 73:..... *(STRUGGLING/FIGHTING SOUNDS)*

Forest Animals:..Wolf, you are wrong. Little Red Riding Hood is very strong.

Red Riding:..........Gran, grab a belt and tie his paws!

Gran:....................*(she ties his paws tight)* Got you! That will teach you to mess with my granddaughter.

Wolf:....................Ok, ok, I give up. I admit it. You are stronger than I am. Let me go and I will tell your Mother.

Red Riding:.........Tell my Mother?!

Wolf:....................It was your Mother who put me up to this.

Red Riding:.........She what?

Wolf:....................She worries that you will get hurt because you think you're so strong. She wanted to scare you so you would be more careful.

Gran:....................So, she asked you to scare Little Red Riding Hood?

Wolf:....................Yes. I'm sorry I locked you in the closet.

Gran:....................It beats being stuck in bed all day.

Red Riding:.........My own Mother! I am shocked!

Wolf:....................Please, could you untie my paws now?

Red Riding:.........If I do let you come with me, you have to tell my Mom how strong I am.

Forest Animals:..The Wolf is being polite. This just doesn't seem right.

SCENE 5: *(Tea Time)*

Narrator: ....Little Red Riding Hood, the Wolf, and Mother are having tea.

Mother:................Really, Wolf. I had hoped you would do better.

Wolf:....................I am sorry. But, your daughter really is strong. She also knew I wasn't your Mother.

Red Riding:.........Mom, I know you did it because you love me. I know I have to be careful. But please, stop calling me little.

Wolf:....................Why not call her Mighty Red Riding Hood?

Mother:................*(sighs)* Very well, but it's a funny name.

Red Riding:.........Thanks, Mom. *(Hugs her)*

Wolf:....................I must go now. Good bye, Mighty Red Riding Hood.

Red Riding:.........Goodbye, Wolf.

Narrator: ....Mother walks the Wolf to the door. She whispers in his ear.

Mother:...............Have you got any brothers and sisters who are... how shall I say it?.... a bit stronger than you?

Forest Animals:...The Wolf will never scare anyone else in the woods. Because now he has to answer to Mighty Red Riding Hood.

THE END

Little Red Riding Hood Prop Patterns

Directions: Copy, color, cut out, and laminate for durability. Cut a strip of construction paper and tape to either side of the night cap so that it fits the child's head comfortably.

Gran's cap—make two, one for Gran and one for the Wolf

Little Red Riding Hood Prop Patterns

Directions: Copy, color, cut out, and laminate for durability Cut out eye holes. Tape a construction paper strip from the left side to the right side of the mask so that it fits the child's head comfortably.

(cut out)   (cut out)

Wolf mask

Directions: Copy, color, cut out, and laminate for durability.

Basket of food

The Elves & The Shoemaker

PERFORMANCE PREPARATION SCRIPT AND PROPS

Characters and Reading Levels

The Elves & The Shoemaker includes five characters and a group choral reading.

- Shoemaker .... reading level 1.8
- Shoemaker's Wife .... reading level 2.5
- Elf 1 .... reading level 2.1
- Elf 2 .... reading level 1.9
- Narrator .... reading level 2.4
- Group Reading: .... reading level 2.2

The group choral reading can be read by a small or a large group—allowing the entire class to participate. You may also choose to eliminate the choral reading. Make a single copy of the script and "white-out" the lines of the group reading. Then, copy the edited script for the five performing story characters.

Reproducible Script and Props

- Reproduce the script: *The Elves & The Shoemaker*, found on pages 70–75 for each student.
- Make the story props—patterns and directions are found on pages 75–77.

Audio CD Sound Effects

- Sound effects for *The Elves & The Shoemaker*, are found on tracks 74–80. Directions for when to play each sound effect can be found in the script.

Optional Costume & Set Suggestions

- Workshop and window: set up low tables where the elves and shoemaker can work. Create a window that the elves can climb in and out. Low bench and display real shoes.
- Shoemaker and his wife should wear aprons.
- Elves: tattered old clothes and stocking caps

READING PREPARATION AND ENRICHMENT ACTIVITIES

Review the Traditional Story

- *The Elves and the Shoemaker* by Jacob Grimm and Jim Lamarche. Chronicle Books (2003)
- *The Elves and the Shoemaker* (Classic Fairy Tale Collection) by John Cech and Kirill Chelushkin. Sterling (2007)
- *The Elves and the Shoemaker* (Ready to Read) by Nick Page, Claire Page, and Sara Baker. Make Believe Ideas (2006)
- *Elves and the Shoemaker* (Flip-Up Fairy Tales) by Alison Edgson. Childs Play Intl Ltd (2007)

Teach New Vocabulary

Teach the following vocabulary (word recognition and meaning) prior to reading the script: *amazing, cottage, curtains, double, easy, elf, elves, fairies, handsome, human, kindness, leather, remember, rewarded, Shoemaker, Shorty, stitch, tonight, workshop.*

Encourage Fluency

- First, read through the script without using any of the props.
- Model fluent reading for the children. This story may not be as familiar as most of the other included fairy tales, so hearing the story prior to reading it will be helpful for many of the children.
- There is a lot of quick and sometimes difficult dialogue in this story. Use peer reading techniques using Scene 2 on pages 70 and 71.

Enrichment Activities

- Have the children pretend to be either the Shoemaker or the Shoemaker's wife and write a thank-you note to the elves for all their help.
- Have the students design a shirt and a pair of shoes for the elves. What would they look like?

Script: The Elves and The Shoemaker

SCENE 1: *(In the Shoemaker's small cottage)*

CD TRACK 74: .... *(MUSIC TO BEGIN THE STORY)*

Narrator: .... This is the Shoemaker's small cottage. It's late at night. The Shoemaker has just cut the leather for a pair of shoes.

Wife: .... Good night, Tom. I'm going to bed.

Shoemaker: .... Good night, Molly. I'll see you soon.

Wife: .... Have you cut out the last pair of shoes?

Shoemaker: .... Yes, I have. We must sell these shoes. We have no more money.

Wife: .... What will we do?

Shoemaker: .... Try not to worry.

Wife: .... That's easy for you to say. How will we eat?

Shoemaker: .... Let's hope we sell the shoes. I will get up early to make them.

Wife: .... Tom, you do make fine shoes.

Shoemaker: .... Thank you. Let's hope you're not the only one who thinks so.

Wife: .... Yes, let's hope.

Group Reading: ..... The poor Shoemaker and his wife! Who will help them?

SCENE 2: *(Late that same night)*

CD TRACK 75: .... *(CREAKING WINDOW OPENS, THEN CLOSES)*

Narrator: .... An Elf climbs in the open window. He leans back out and talks to someone else.

Elf 1: .... *(whispering)* He's gone to bed. Come on!

Elf 2: .... *(voice comes from outside window)* I can't help it if my legs are short. It's easy for you—your legs are so long! You don't look like an elf!

Elf 1: .... Hush! We've got work to do. Poor Tom, he needs our help. He has to sell these shoes.

Elf 2:..................He is the best shoemaker in the land. Why does he need our help?

Elf 1:..................He may be the best shoemaker. But, shoes made by elves are even better. You're an elf, you know that.

Elf 2:..................Yes, I do, but I like to hear you say it. It makes me feel good.

Elf 1:..................When a human sees a pair of shoes made by an elf, they have to buy them. It's as if the shoes have a spell on them.

Elf 2:..................Does that mean I'm kind of magic?

Elf 1:..................Yes, it does. Even if you have very short legs.

Elf 2:..................Will you stop talking about my legs?

Elf 1:..................Ok, Shorty, let's get to work. The Shoemaker needs our help. We've got a pair of shoes to make.

Elf 2:..................Can I make the right shoe?

Elf 1:..................Ok. I'll make the left shoe.

Elf 2:..................One more thing.

Elf 1:..................Yes?

Elf 2:..................Please, don't call me Shorty.

Elf 1:..................Ok. Now work!

    CD TRACK 76:.......*(HAMMERING SOUNDS)*

Group Reading:.....Two little elves. Can they really help Tom and Molly?

<u>**SCENE 3:**</u> *(The next morning)*

Narrator:................The next morning Tom comes into the workshop. He sees a pair of shoes on the table.

Shoemaker:............Molly! Come here!

Wife:......................I'm coming. What's all the fuss about?

Shoemaker:............Look! Look at these. They're the best shoes I've ever seen.

Wife:......................*(laughing)* You are getting a big head!

Shoemaker:............No, you don't get it. I didn't make them.

Wife:......................You must have.

Shoemaker:	But, I didn't. I came in and here they were.
Wife:	*(looks at them closely)* You're right. Even you can't stitch this well.
Shoemaker:	So, who could have done it?
Wife:	The fairies? I don't know.
Group Reading:	Well, the two little elves worked hard. But, will it be enough to really help Tom and Molly.

SCENE 4: *(Later that day)*

Narrator:	It was later that same day.
CD TRACK 77:	*(CASH REGISTER)*
Shoemaker:	Molly! I've just sold the shoes. A man with fine clothes came in. He saw the shoes and said he had to have them.
Wife:	What did he pay for them?
Shoemaker:	More than I asked him for! He gave me double.
Wife:	Now, you can buy leather for two pairs of shoes.
Group Reading:	The little elves did help! Will they help Tom and Molly again?

SCENE 5: *(Later that week)*

Narrator:	The elves have come every night for a week. They have worked very hard.
Elf 1:	Come on, Shorty. We need to work fast! We have to make four pairs of shoes tonight.
Elf 2:	Don't call me Shorty!
Elf 1:	Tom is doing well. He must have sold six pairs of shoes this week.
Elf 2:	And, there's food in the house! Flowers on the table.
Elf 1:	You can be proud, Shorty. We have done good work and helped a good man.
Elf 2:	I do feel proud, but don't call me Shorty. How long do we keep coming?

Elf 1: ....We will know when its time to stop. Let's work now.

CD TRACK 78: ....*(HAMMERING SOUNDS)*

Group Reading: ......Two little elves made six pairs of shoes. Will Tom and Molly find out who is helping them?

SCENE 6: *(The next day)*

Narrator: ....It is the next day, Tom and his wife are eating lunch.

Wife:.......................We have to find out who helps us every night.

Shoemaker: ....You're right. We have food and money now.

Wife:.......................Let's hide in the workshop tonight. Then, we can see who it is.

Shoemaker: ....Good idea. We can stand behind the curtains. We have to be quiet.

Wife:.......................You won't hear a peep out of me.

Group Reading: ......Will Tom and Molly see the elves? Will the elves see Tom and Molly?

SCENE 7: *(Molly and Tom hiding behind the curtain)*

Narrator: ....Molly and Tom are hiding behind the curtains.

Wife:.......................*(whispering)* I can't stay here much longer. My back is killing me.

Shoemaker: ....SShhh. No one will come if they hear us.

Wife:.......................Five more minutes, then I'm off to bed.

Shoemaker: ....SSSShhhhh! Look! The window!

Narrator: ....The elves are climbing in through the window. They run to the table and start working.

Elf 1: ....We will make seven pairs tonight. He must be getting good money for our shoes!

Elf 2: ....Good! It's getting colder now. I like it when I have to work fast. It warms me up!

Elf 1: ....I know what you mean. Winter will be here soon. Our clothes are not very warm. Chop chop, Shorty! Get working.

Elf 2:.............I will, but please don't call me Shorty.

CD TRACK 79:.......*(HAMMERING SOUNDS)*

Group Reading:.....The elves are working faster than before. Can they make seven pairs of shoes?

SCENE 8: *(The next night)*

Narrator:................The next night, Tom and Molly put out the tiny clothes and shoes they made for the elves.

Wife:....................Do you think they will be pleased with the new clothes I made, and the shoes you made?

Shoemaker:............They will love them. Those poor elves wore thin rags.

Wife:....................I wish we could do more.

Shoemaker:...........We had better hide. They will be here soon.

Narrator:................Molly and Tom hide behind the curtains. Soon, the elves climb in. They see the new clothes and shoes on the table.

Elf 1:......................Look! They must be for us!

Elf 2::.....................Are you sure?

Elf 1:......................Who else do they know our size, silly?

Elf 2:.....................*(tearful)* I've never had real clothes.

Elf 1:......................They're the finest elf clothes I've ever seen.

Elf 2:.....................Can we put them on now?

Elf 1:......................Sure. *(picks up pair of trousers)* Here, you take these.

Elf 2:.....................But they're for you.

Elf 1:......................Why do you say that?

Elf 2:.....................They are the longest pair. They are for you. I'm Shorty, remember?

Elf 1:......................Can't you tell? You are bigger. If an elf does well on his first job, he will grow to full size. That's what you have done.

Elf 2:.....................*(tearful)* This is the best day of my life.

Elf 1:......................Come on then. We look amazing. Let's go and find a party.

Elf 2:.....................What about the shoes?

Elf 1: ....The Shoemaker doesn't need us any more. He'll be just fine.

CD TRACK 80: ....*(CREAKING WINDOW OPENS, THEN CLOSES)*

Narrator: ....The elves climb out of the window. Then, Tom and Molly come out from hiding.

Wife: ....Did you hear that?

Shoemaker: ....What?

Wife: ....They are going to find a party! I'm not sure I want my little clothes at a party. They might get dirty.

Shoemaker: ....But, they are not our clothes. It was our gift to the elves.

Wife: ....I guess you are right. They did look handsome, didn't they?

Shoemaker: ....Very. I must go to bed. I have shoes to make in the morning. It will feel good to be the shoemaker again.

Group Reading: .....By making shoes, the elves saved Tom and Molly. By making clothes, Tom and Molly saved the elves from being cold. True kindness is always rewarded.

THE END

The Elves and the Shoemaker Prop Patterns

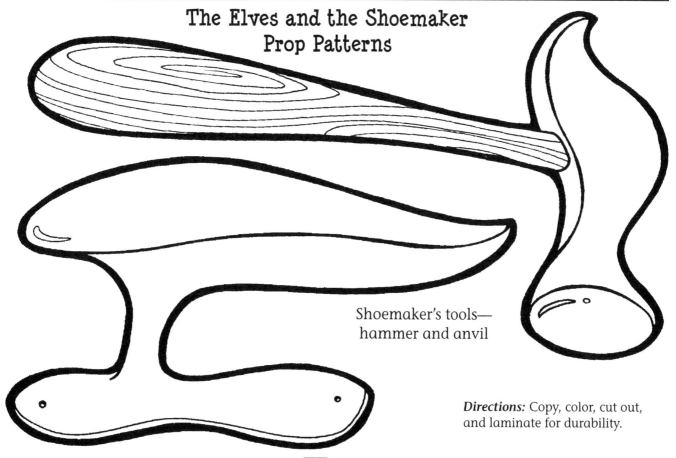

Shoemaker's tools—
hammer and anvil

Directions: Copy, color, cut out, and laminate for durability.

The Elves and the Shoemaker Prop Patterns

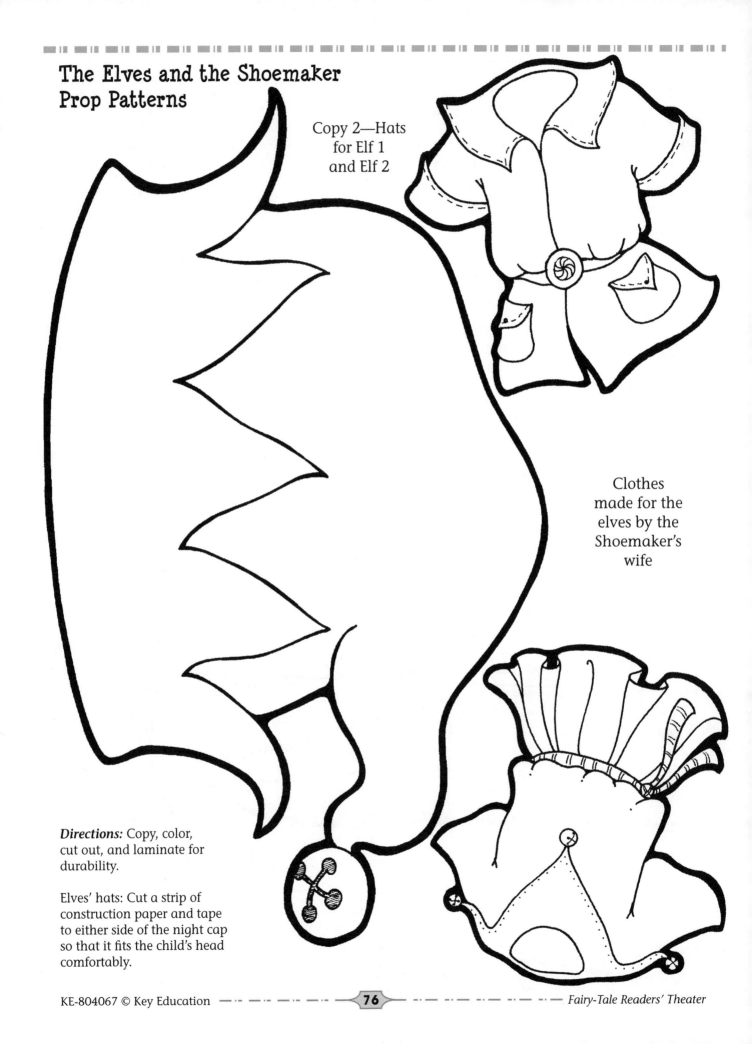

Copy 2—Hats for Elf 1 and Elf 2

Clothes made for the elves by the Shoemaker's wife

Directions: Copy, color, cut out, and laminate for durability.

Elves' hats: Cut a strip of construction paper and tape to either side of the night cap so that it fits the child's head comfortably.

Shoes

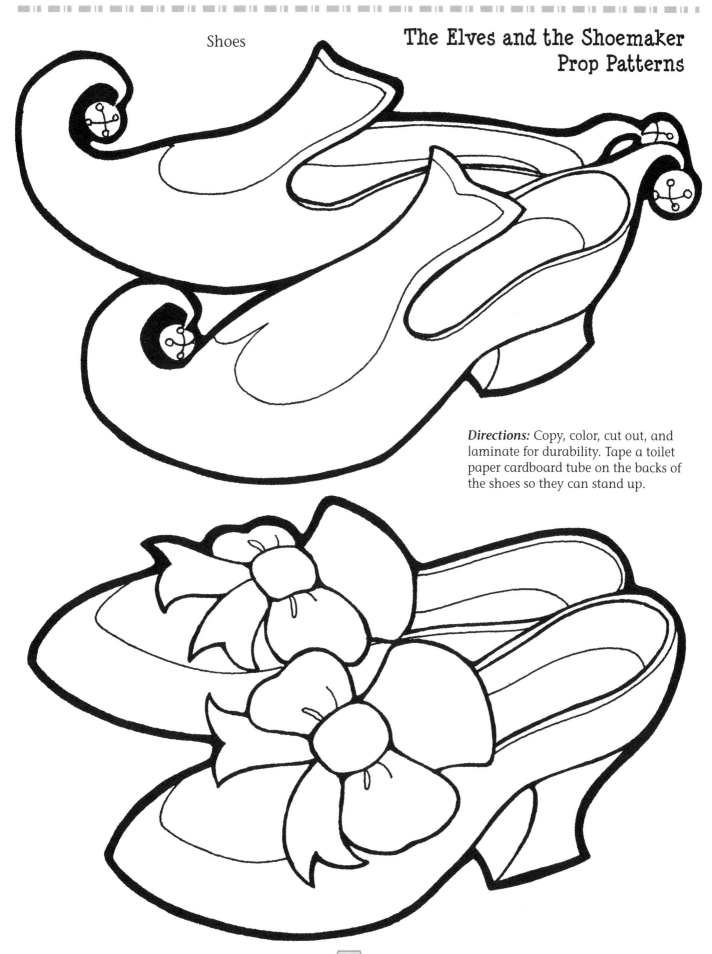

Directions: Copy, color, cut out, and laminate for durability. Tape a toilet paper cardboard tube on the backs of the shoes so they can stand up.

Cinderella

PERFORMANCE PREPARATION SCRIPT AND PROPS

Characters and Reading Levels

Cinderella includes seven characters and a group choral reading.

- ◆ Cinderella .... reading level 1.9
- ◆ Stepmother................ reading level 2.4
- ◆ Ugly Sister 1 .... reading level 2.0
- ◆ Ugly Sister 2 .... reading level 2.1
- ◆ Fairy Godmother....... reading level 2.1
- ◆ Prince .... reading level 2.1
- ◆ Narrator .... reading level 2.5
- ◆ Mice (group) .... reading level 1.6

The "Mice" choral reading can be read by a small or a large group—allowing the entire class to participate. You may also choose to eliminate the choral reading. Make a single copy of the script and "white-out" the lines of the "Mice." Then, copy the edited script for the seven performing story characters.

Reproducible Script and Props

- ◆ Reproduce the script: *Cinderella,* found on pages 79–84 for each student.
- ◆ Make the story props—patterns and directions are found on pages 84–86.

Audio CD Sound Effects

- ◆ Sound effects for *Cinderella,* are found on tracks 81–86. Directions for when to play each sound effect can be found in the script.

Optional Costume & Set Suggestions

- ◆ Cinderella: old dirty outfit and a nice long dress; broom, cleaning rags.
- ◆ Stepsisters: long dresses; lots of jewelry, very over done.
- ◆ Stepmother: long dark dress.
- ◆ Fairy Godmother: white or pastel long dress; magic wand.
- ◆ Prince: white shirt; black pants; colorful sash tied across chest; crown.
- ◆ Mice: enlarge the patterns on page 84 and copy as many as needed for the students. Attach a tongue depressor and use as puppets.

READING PREPARATION AND ENRICHMENT ACTIVITIES

Review the Traditional Story

- ◆ *Cinderella Outgrows the Glass Slipper and Other Zany Fractured Fairy Tale Plays* by Joan M. Wolf. Scholastic Professional Books (2002)
- ◆ *The Egyptian Cinderella* by Shirley Climo and Ruth Heller. HarperTrophy (1992)
- ◆ *Cindy Ellen: A Wild Western Cinderella* by Susan Lowell and Jane K. Manning. HarperTrophy (2001)
- ◆ *Cinderella* by Charles Perrault, Amy Ehrlich, and Susan Jeffers. Puffin (1993)
- ◆ *James Marshall's Cinderella* by Barbara Karlin and James Marshall. Puffin (2001)

Teach New Vocabulary

Teach the following vocabulary (word recognition and meaning) prior to reading the script: *angry, brother, carriage, Cinderella, fault, Fairy Godmother, grumpy, midnight, palace, prince, princess, quick, slipper, stain, stepmother, toenails, ugly, unkind, untidy, visit.*

Encourage Fluency

- ◆ First, read through the script without using any of the props.
- ◆ The mice could speak with high-pitched "mouse-like" voices. The mice are either very excited and happy or very sad and worried.
- ◆ Have the children record the script after only reading it once or twice. Then, record them after several days of practice. Discuss the fluency difference in the two recordings.

Enrichment Activities

- ◆ Compare and contrast: This version has a very different ending than most of the traditional versions. Compare and contract how the endings are different.
- ◆ Reading details: Make a list of everything that happened at the ball. *(See page 81, Scene 4.)*

Script: Cinderella

SCENE 1: *(In Cinderella's kitchen)*

CD TRACK 81:..... *(MUSIC TO BEGIN THE STORY)*

Stepmother:.... Girls, come here! Quick! Quick! Quick!

Ugly Sister 1:.. What is it, Mother?

Ugly Sister 2:.. It's a letter! Who's it from?

Stepmother:.... It's from the Palace. The King is having a Ball for the Prince. He wants to find the Prince a wife!

Ugly Sister 1:.. Me, me, me! Let it be me, me, me!

Ugly Sister 2:.. No! Me, me, me! Let it be me, me, me!

Narrator:........ Cinderella comes into the room with a broom. She is dirty and tired.

Cinderella:...... Why are you so happy?

Stepmother:.... My girls are going to the Prince's party.

Cinderella:...... May I go?

Ugly Sister 1:.. You have nothing to wear.

Ugly Sister 2:.. And even if you did, you're not pretty.

Ugly Sister 1:.. Not pretty like me, me, me!

Ugly Sister 2:.. Nor pretty like me, me, me!

Mice:............... Poor Cinderella! Poor pretty Cinderella!

SCENE 2: *(It's the night of the Ball)*

Narrator:........ The sisters are about to leave for the Ball. Cinderella is sweeping the floor.

Stepmother:.... Girls, make sure you spend lots of time with the Prince.

Ugly Sister 1:.. He'll want to talk to me all night, won't he, Mommy? I look lovely, don't I, Mommy?

Ugly Sister 2:.. I do, too—don't I, Mommy?

Stepmother:.... You both look pretty as can be. I don't know how the Prince will choose between you.

CD TRACK 82:..... *(HORSE AND CARRIAGE SOUNDS)*

Ugly Sister 1: .. Here's our carriage now! Bye, bye, Mommy.

Ugly Sister 2: .. Bye, Bye, Mommy.

Stepmother:.... Bye, bye, my two Bunny Kins.

Narrator: .... The stepmother waves goodbye to the girls. Then, she looks at Cinderella.

Stepmother:.... What are you staring at? Get on with your work. Then, go to your room. I don't want to look at you at all tonight. *(leaves the room)*

Cinderella:...... *(to herself)* It's not fair. I wish I could go to the Ball.

CD TRACK 83:..... *(FLASH AND BOOM, FAIRY GODMOTHER APPEARS)*

Narrator: .... Suddenly, there's a flash of light and a loud bang. The Fairy Godmother is standing in the room.

Godmother:.... Cinderella! You shall go to the Ball!

Mice: .... Hooray, Cinderella! Hooray, pretty Cinderella is going to the Ball!

SCENE 3: *(An hour later)*

Narrator: .... In only an hour, Cinderella is ready to go to the ball.

Cinderella:...... Thank you so much, Fairy Godmother!

Godmother:.... Don't forget to be home by midnight. If you stay later, your dress will turn to rags. Your horses will turn to mice. And, your carriage will turn to a pumpkin.

Cinderella:...... *(getting into carriage)* I won't. Thank you.

Godmother:.... Have fun, dear.

CD TRACK 84:..... *(HORSE AND CARRIAGE SOUNDS)*

Mice: .... Home by midnight, Cinderella! Don't be late, pretty Cinderella!

<u>SCENE 4:</u> *(Back at Cinderella's home)*

Narrator: .... The ugly sisters have arrived home. They are very grumpy. The Stepmother is very angry. And, Cinderella is back in her rags, cleaning.

Stepmother: .... You didn't talk to the Prince at all?

Ugly Sister 1: .. We tried, we tried all night.

Ugly Sister 2: .. He only wanted to dance with one girl.

Ugly Sister 1: .. I pushed her out of the way twice. But, the Prince went after her.

Ugly Sister 2: ...And I put wine on her dress and it didn't stain. It was like magic.

Stepmother: .... Who was this awful girl?

Ugly Sister 1: .. We don't know. No one knew who she was.

Ugly Sister 2: .. At midnight, she ran away.

Stepmother: .... Why didn't you talk to the Prince then?

Ugly Sister 1: .. He told us to leave.

Ugly Sister 2: .. I tried to give him a hug.

Ugly Sister 1: .. And I asked him for a dance.

Stepmother: .... And? *(they look at the floor.)* Well? What did he say? *(The two sisters look at the floor)* Tell me girls!

Ugly Sister 1: .. *(mutters)* He yelled at us.

Ugly Sister 2: .. He told us to go and leave him alone.

Stepmother: .... How dare he! How dare he speak to my girls like that! Who does he think he is?

Cinderella: .... *(a dreamy smile on her face)* A Prince can dance with any girl he likes.

Stepmother: .... Oh, be quiet!

Ugly Sister 1: .. Oh, be quiet!

Ugly Sister 2: .. Oh, be quiet!

Mice: .... Poor, Cinderella! Poor, pretty Cinderella!

SCENE 5: *(Two days later)*

Narrator: .... It is morning, two days later.

Ugly Sister 1: .. Mommy! How long before the Prince arrives?

Stepmother: .... Five minutes.

Ugly Sister 2: .. Have I got time to cut my toenails again? It might make my feet smaller.

Ugly Sister 1: .. I'm just going to curl my toes up.

Cinderella: ...... It will never fit you. It is not your shoe.

Ugly Sister 1: .. It's not our fault that silly girl ran away.

Cinderella: ...... But it's the girl he fell in love with. He's looking for her.

Ugly Sister 2: .. Oh, Cinderella! He could easily fall in love with one of us!

Stepmother: .... Cinderella, when the Prince comes, stay out of the room. You will make it look untidy. Got it?

Cinderella: ...... *(sighing)* Yes, Stepmother.

Mice: .... Poor, Cinderella! Poor, pretty Cinderella!

SCENE 6: *(Prince at Cinderella's home)*

Narrator: .... The Prince is watching the first sister as she tries to push her foot into the slipper.

Prince: .... Give it up. It's never going to fit.

Ugly Sister 1: .. It's nearly there, just give me a minute.

Prince: .... No! I'm sorry. You are not the girl I'm looking for. No way! Give me back the slipper.

Ugly Sister 2: .. My turn!

Prince: .... *(to himself)* On no! It's her!

Ugly Sister 2: .. It fits my big toe. Look!

Prince: .... We really must go. We have many houses to visit.

   CD TRACK 85: ..... *(FOOTSTEPS RUNNING)*

Narrator: .... Suddenly, Cinderella runs in.

Cinderella: ...... May I try?

Stepmother:.... What?!

Ugly Sister 1: .. You?

Ugly Sister 2: . Not you!

Cinderella:...... Please, let me try.

Prince:............. *(studying her face)* Yes, let her.

Narrator: .... Cinderella slips on the glass shoe. Then, she takes the other shoe from her pocket.

Prince:............. It is you! But why do you live with these ugly sisters? Why are you dressed in rags?

Cinderella:...... Ask my Stepmother.

Prince:............. Well? Why are you so unkind to her?

Stepmother:.... Well, Prince, I, errrr. . . *(bursts into tears)*

Ugly Sister 1: .. Go on Mommy, tell him. Or he'll just think you are mean.

Ugly Sister 2: .. Yes, tell them Mommy.

Cinderella:...... Tell us what? What's going on?

Stepmother:.... *(sniffs)* Cinderella looks so like her dad. I miss him so much. Every time I see her, it makes me so sad.

Cinderella:....... *(amazed)* So, you don't hate me?

Stepmother:.... You poor girl. I'm sorry. This has been so unfair to you.

Prince:............. Yes, it has. Will you be nice to her now?

Stepmother:.... Yes.

Prince:............. *(looks at sisters)* And you two?

Ugly Sisters:.... Yes.

Prince:............. Good. I'm taking Cinderella to the Palace to tell my father we are getting married. *(looks at Cinderella)* You do want to marry me, don't you?

Cinderella:...... You bet I do!

Prince:............. Great! The rest of you can come to the Palace for dinner. Come at five.

Stepmother/Ugly Sisters:.....Yes, Prince!

Narrator: .... The Prince and Cinderella leave for the Palace. They wave good-bye.

CD TRACK 86: ..... *(HORSE AND CARRIAGE SOUNDS)*

Stepmother: .... What a surprise!

Ugly Sister 1: .. Cinderella's going to marry the Prince!

Ugly Sister 2: .. We're having dinner at the Palace!

Ugly Sister 1: .. Mommy?

Stepmother: .... Yes.

Ugly Sister 2: .. I know what you're going to ask.

Stepmother: .... What?!

Ugly Sisters: .... Has the Prince got any brothers?

Mice: .... Hooray for Princess Cinderella! Pretty Princess Cinderella!

THE END

Cinderella Prop Patterns

Directions: Copy, color, cut out, and laminate for durability. Cut a toilet paper cardboard tube in half. Tape it on the backs of the mice so they can stand up.

Cinderella's mice

Cinderella Prop Patterns

Directions: Copy, color, cut out, and laminate for durability.

Invitation to the
Royal Ball

Glass slipper
Make 2, one for the
Prince to carry and the
other one for Cinderella
to put in her pocket.

Cinderella Prop Patterns

Directions: Copy, color, cut out, and laminate for durability.

pumpkin

Directions:
Copy, color, cut out and laminate for durability. Glue on sequins and plastic "jewels." Tape to a plastic headband or staple a construction paper strip so that it fit's the child's head.

Prince's crown

Snow White & the Seven Dwarfs

PERFORMANCE PREPARATION SCRIPT AND PROPS

Characters and Reading Levels

Snow White & the Seven Dwarfs **includes eleven characters and a group choral reading.**

- Snow White .... reading level 2.1
- Stepmother/Queen ..... reading level 2.0
- Doc .... reading level 1.7
- Bashful .... reading level 1.9
- Happy .... reading level 1.8
- Sneezy .... reading level 2.0
- Sleepy .... reading level 1.9
- Grumpy .... reading level 1.7
- Dopey .... reading level 2.0
- Prince .... reading level 2.2
- Narrator .... reading level 2.2
- Squirrels (group) .... reading level 1.9

The "squirrels" choral reading can be read by a small or a large group—allowing the entire class to participate. You may also choose to eliminate the choral reading. Make a single copy of the script and "white-out" the lines of the "squirrels." Then, copy the edited script for the seven performing story characters.

Reproducible Script and Props

- Reproduce the script: *Snow White & The Seven Dwarfs,* found on pages 88–93 for each student.
- Make the story props—patterns and directions are found on pages 94–96.

Audio CD Sound Effects

- Sound effects for *Snow White & the Seven Dwarfs,* are found on tracks 87–98. Directions for when to play each sound effect can be found in the script.

Optional Costume & Set Suggestions

- Dwarfs: stocking caps and white shirts with names printed on the front of the shirts.
- Snow White: long dress
- Queen: black dress
- Prince: white shirt; black pants; colorful sash tied across chest; crown.

READING PREPARATION AND ENRICHMENT ACTIVITIES

Review the Traditional Story

- *Snow White* by Jacob Ludwig Carl Grimm, Wilhelm Grimm, and Charles Santore. Random House Books for Young Readers (2004)
- *Snow White and the Seven Dwarfs: A Fairy Tale by the Brothers Grimm* by Myriam Deru. Abbeville Kids (2001)
- *Walt Disney's Snow White and the Seven Dwarfs* by Lara Bergen. Disney Press (2005)
- *Snow White and the Seven Dwarfs* by Belinda Downes. DK Children (2002)
- *Snow-White and the Seven Dwarfs* by Jacob Grimm. Farrar, Straus and Giroux (1987)

Teach New Vocabulary

Teach the following vocabulary (word recognition and meaning) prior to reading the script: *Bashful, bury, coffin, combs, Dopey, Dwarfs, evil, fairest, Grumpy, journey, lovely, Queen, returning, safe, Sleepy, Sneezy, squirrels, stepmother, witch, worst, worth.*

Encourage Fluency

- First, read through the script without using any of the props.
- Each dwarf should choose a unique voice—a voice that reflects the dwarf's name such as, Sneezy could sneeze after each line; Sleepy could yawn while he talks; Grumpy could always sound "grumpy," etc.
- The squirrels always sound like they are warning Snow White. They should sound frantic.

Enrichment Activities

- Write a description of each of the Dwarfs. How are they alike? How are they different?
- Snow White is comical in this version. Make a list of the things that Snow White is good at and the things she is not good at.

Script: Snow White & the Seven Dwarfs

SCENE 1: *(In the dwarfs' cottage)*

CD TRACK 87: ..... *(MUSIC TO BEGIN THE STORY)*

Grumpy: .... We said she could stay if she cooked for us. And she kept the house nice.

Dopey: .... She was so happy when we said that.

Doc: .... And she's tried so hard.

Happy: .... She's cooked every night.

Bashful: .... And she's washed up.

Sneezy: .... And cleaned.

Sleepy: .... And tidied up.

Grumpy: .... But it's not working, is it?

Dopey: .... Let's face it—she hasn't got a clue!

Doc: .... I can't eat the food she cooks.

Happy: .... The plates are still dirty after she's washed them.

Bashful: .... I can't find anything.

Sneezy: .... She puts clothes in the stove and plates in the closet.

Sleepy: .... But, she is so lovely.

Grumpy: .... So kind.

Dopey: .... So pretty.

Doc: .... She tries so hard.

Happy: .... She's a princess. She's never done any of these things before.

Bashful: .... That's right. She'll get better at it.

Sneezy: .... I don't care if the house is a mess. And I don't care if the food is terrible.

Sleepy: .... We just want her safe from her evil stepmother.

Grumpy: .... When we are out, she must never open the door.

SCENE 2: *(The next day)*

Narrator: .... It is the next day. Snow White is alone in the house. The Queen is dressed as an old woman and knocks at the door.

CD TRACK 88: ..... *(KNOCKING AT DOOR)*

Snow White: ... *(shouts through door)* Hello? Who is it?

Queen: .... I sell combs for lovely hair!

Snow White: ... I'm sorry. The Dwarfs told me not to open the door.

Queen: .... The Dwarfs would like you to have a treat. Please, let me in. What harm can an old lady do?

Squirrels: .... Don't open the door, Snow White! Don't open the door!

Snow White: ... You are right. They do tell me that no one has hair as lovely as mine.

CD TRACK 89: ..... *(DOOR OPENS, THEN CLOSES)*

Narrator: .... Snow White lets the witch in.

Queen: .... Now my dear, let me put these combs in your hair.

Narrator: .... The witch puts the combs in Snow White's hair. Snow White drops to the floor.

CD TRACK 90: ..... *(FALLING TO THE FLOOR)*

Queen: .... No one has hair as lovely as yours? Well, not anymore! *(She leaves, laughing.)*

Squirrels: .... You should not have opened the door, Snow White! You should not have opened the door!

SCENE 3: *(The dwarfs return from work)*

Narrator: .... The Dwarfs are returning from work.

CD TRACK 91: ..... *(DOOR OPENS, THEN CLOSES, FOOTSTEPS RUNNING)*

Grumpy: .... Snow White!

Dopey: .... Is she dead?

Doc: .... What's that in her hair?

Happy: .... Pull it out! Quick!

Bashful: .... *(pulls out the comb)* Ouch! It burns.

Sleepy: .... It must have a bad spell cast on it.

Sneezy: .... Look! She's waking up.

Snow White: ... Where am I? Why am I on the floor?

Grumpy: .... The Queen must have tried to kill you.

Dopey: .... We told you not to open the door.

Squirrels: .... You should not have opened the door, Snow White! You should not have opened the door!

Doc: .... She was sure to find out where you live.

Snow White: ... It wasn't my stepmother. It was a little old lady.

Happy: .... It must have been your stepmother.

Bashful: .... She just looked like a little old lady.

Sneezy: .... Never, never, never, open the door.

Sleepy: .... Are you alright now, Snow White?

Snow White: ... Yes, I'm fine. And I've cooked you a treat—fried peas and boiled toast!

Sneezy: .... Oh, you shouldn't have.

Squirrels: .... Listen to the Dwarfs, Snow White! Listen to the Dwarfs!

SCENE 4: *(The next day)*

Narrator: .... It is the next day. The Dwarfs are out at work. The Queen knocks at the door.

CD TRACK 92: ..... *(KNOCKING AT DOOR)*

Snow White: ... *(shouts through the door)* Hello? Who is it?

Queen: .... A poor old woman selling the best apples in the world.

Snow White: ... I do love apples, but I can't let you in. The Dwarfs have told me not to.

Queen: .... But they love you so much. They would want you to eat my lovely apples.

Snow White: ... You might be my evil stepmother trying to kill me. All because I am more lovely than she is.

Queen: .... Let me in and I'll eat half the apple. Then, you'll know it can't hurt you.

Snow White:... Maybe you're right. They do say I should eat more. *(She lets her in)*

Squirrels: .... Don't open the door, Snow White! Don't open the door!

CD TRACK 93: ..... *(DOOR OPENS, THEN CLOSES)*

Queen: .... *(bites into the apple and gives the other half to Snow White)* Now taste it. See how good it is!

Narrator: .... Snow White bites into the apple and falls to the floor.

CD TRACK 94: ..... *(FALLING TO THE FLOOR)*

Queen: .... Now, let's see who's the fairest of all. *(Queen leaves, laughing)*

Squirrels: .... You should not have opened the door, Snow White! You should not have opened the door!

SCENE 5: *(The Dwarfs return home from work)*

Narrator: .... The Dwarfs return from work and find Snow White on the floor.

Dopey:............. Snow White!

Sneezy:........... Not again!

Bashful: .... What should we do?

Doc:................. I think she's dead!

Grumpy: .... Her heart is not beating!

Happy:............ She's gone!

Sleepy:............. We can't save her. In the morning we'll have to bury her.

Squirrels: .... You should not have opened the door, Snow White! You should not have opened the door!

CD TRACK 95: ..... *(MANY CRYING)*

SCENE 6: *(The next day)*

Narrator: .... The next day, the Dwarfs get ready to bury Snow White.

Sneezy: .... This is the worst day of my life.

Bashful: .... Hang on! We can't bury her.

Doc: .... Why not?

Grumpy: .... Look at her! Her cheeks are still pink.

Happy: .... *(touches her)* Feel her!

Sleepy: .... *(touches her)* She's not cold!

Dopey: .... Let's put her in a glass coffin. Then we can watch over her.

SCENE 7: *(A few days later)*

Narrator: .... A few days later the Prince knocks at the door.

CD TRACK 96: ..... *(KNOCKING AT DOOR)*

Sleepy: .... Don't answer it!

Dopey: .... No! We don't want the Queen to get her hands on Snow White's body.

Grumpy: .... We don't know it's her.

Happy: .... Let me look out of the window.

Bashful: .... Who is it?

Happy: .... Looks like some sort of prince to me.

Sneezy: .... *(shouts through the door)* Who are you and what do you want?

Prince: .... I'm a prince on a long journey. All I need is a glass of water.

Sleepy: .... I say we let him in. We can't live as if we are in a prison.

All Dwarfs: ..... Let him in.

Narrator: .... They let in the Prince. He walks over to the glass coffin.

Prince: .... Who is this? How did she die? Why is she in your home like this?

Bashful: .... She is Snow White. Her evil stepmother killed her.

Happy: .... But, she is still warm. Her cheeks are still pink.

Dopey: .... That's why we didn't bury her.

Doc:............... Maybe there's a way to wake her up.

Prince:............ I wonder....

Sneezy:........... What?

Grumpy:......... Have you got an idea?

Prince:............ I've heard that the kiss of a prince can sometimes do the trick. Worth a try, don't you think?

Dwarfs:........... Yes!

Narrator:........ The Dwarfs picked up the coffin lid. The Prince kisses Snow White. Her eyes open and she sits up.

    CD TRACK 97:..... *(KISSING)*

Snow White:... Where am I? Who are you?

Prince:............ It seems that I am your prince.

Snow White:... Really? How very nice. Are we going to get married?

Prince:............ Would you like to? I'm up for it.

Snow White:... Me, too! I've always wanted to marry a prince. But wait! I can't leave the Dwarfs. They saved my life. I can't leave. They need me to cook and clean up.

Grumpy:......... Nonsense!

Doc:............... You must go!

Happy:........... We'll miss you, of course.

Bashful:.......... And your fried peas.

Sneezy:........... Your boiled toast.

Dopey:............ Your beans with jam.

Sleepy:............ But we'll cope.

Snow White:... You're being so brave and kind. But even if I have my Prince and my Palace, I shall come and cook for you once a week.

Prince:............ Snow White, you are the kindest, sweetest woman alive. Will you cook for me, too?

Snow White:... Every day, my Prince, every day.

Squirrels:........ Ohhh! There is nothing better than a fairy tale with a happy ending!

    CD TRACK 98:..... *(MUSIC TO END THE STORY)*   **THE END**

Directions: Copy, color, cut out, and laminate for durability. Tape a construction paper strip to each side of the cap so that it fits the child's head comfortably.

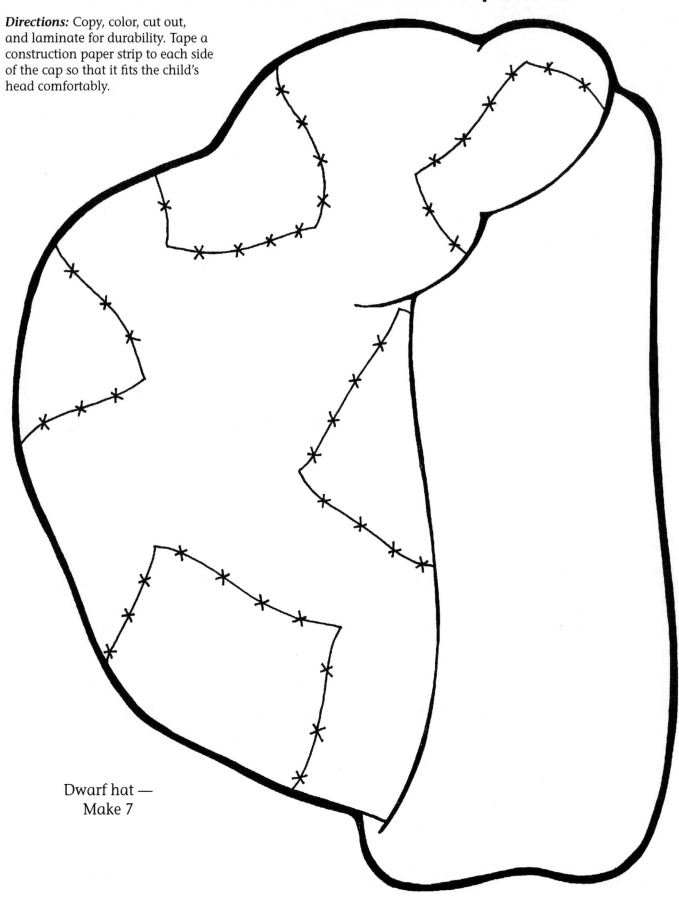

Dwarf hat —
Make 7

Snow White and the Seven Dwarfs Prop Patterns

Directions: Copy, color, cut out, and laminate for durability. Tape a construction paper strip to each side of the cap so that it fits the child's head comfortably.

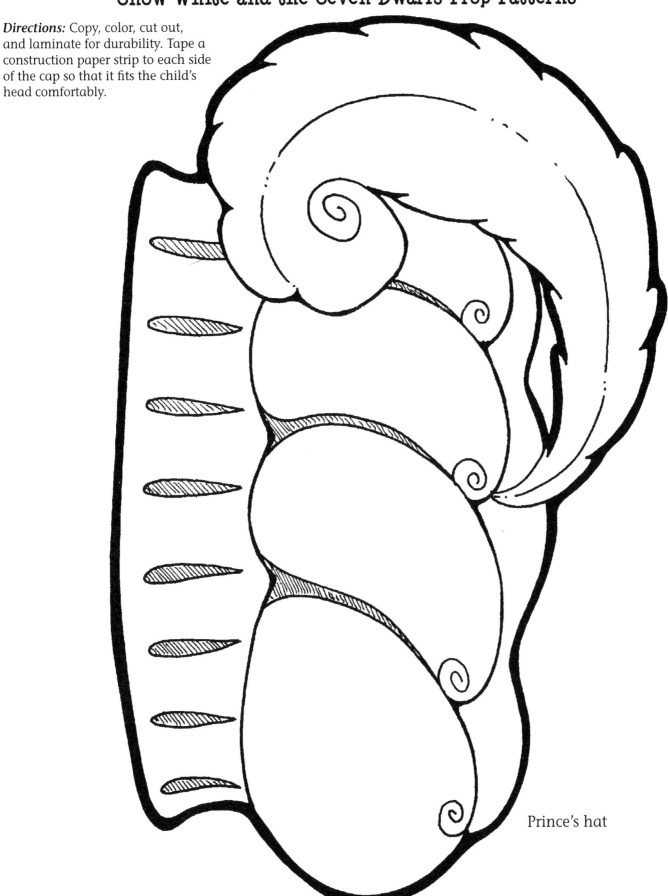

Prince's hat

Snow White and the Seven Dwarfs Prop Patterns

Directions: Copy, color, cut out, and laminate for durability. Cut out eye holes. Tape a construction paper strip from the left side to the right side of the mask so that it fits the child's head comfortably.

Queen's disguise as the old lady

(cut out)

(cut out)